No Fat Fudge

FOREVER CHANGING THE WAY AMERICA MAKES FUDGE

QUICK AND SIMPLE

GREAT FUDGES WITH JUST NO FAT

CREATE YOUR OWN SIGNATURE FUDGE

SEE
"FOR LITTLE HANDS"
A TRADITION IN THE MAKING

by

NORMAN ROSE

On The Cover

An assortment of fat free fudges are seen matched with
a home grown rose called Mr. Lincoln.

First published in the United States of America in 1994 by Norman Rose.
7128 Cedar, Prairie Village, Kansas, 66208.

Edited by Warren Walker

Photographs by Steve White

Photographs Styled by Brenda Rose

Calligraphy by Michael Sull

ISBN 0-9631847-5-X

"How wonderful! Intense flavor, satisfying smooth texture plus no fat."

Mary Hanlon, Liberty, Missouri

"An extra treat, so smooth and delicious. I loved it so and didn't feel guilty eating it. I'm a sweet lover and it's so satisfying."

Donna Cox, Kansas City, Missouri

"An extraordinary book! Great recipes and great fudge."

Sylvia Hunt, Las Cruces, New Mexico

"This fudge is absolutely excellent! It is delicious and smooth in texture. Any no fat food has health benefits."

Shirley Grout, Kansas City, Missouri

"Unbelieveable! The Bon Bons are so good."

Joyce Payne, Basehor, Kansas

"Great fudge on my first try and better fudge on my second try! Simply amazing, with no fat."

Ron Smith, St. Louis, Missouri

"This fudge is truly amazing! I can serve a plate of rich, smooth, no-fat fudge in a variety of colors, flavors and textures. It is a wonderful gift."

Susan Hetrick, Leawood, Kansas

Holiday Fudge, Bon Bons, & Truffles
With Just No Fat   Page 51

Coconut-Rum-Raisin Fudge
Page 122

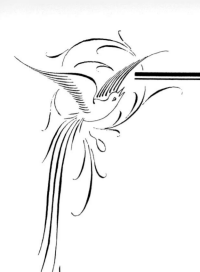

CONTENTS

AUTHOR'S NOTE

This book on no-fat fudge is the latest result of my determination to eat all the things that everybody else is eating, but without the fat.

In my third book, Favorite Foods - No Fat Cooking, (WRS Publishing, Waco, Texas) I tackle what I refer to as "regular food for regular people." For over a year I immersed myself in developing no-fat recipes for everyday food which resulted in over 400 recipes, including favorites such as sausage gravy (perfect gravy every time, guaranteed), pizza, cheesecake, twice-baked potatoes, medium rare prime rib, and homemade bread. But 400 recipes only touches the surface of no-fat cooking possibilities. Lately I've become very excited about tackling fudge, a snack that many of my friends told me couldn't be adapted to no-fat cooking. The result is this book on no-fat fudge. I even resolved to develop peanut butter fudge, because it was one of my favorites before I swore off fatty foods completely. In all candor, the no-fat peanut butter fudge on page 105 is more delicious than any store-bought fat fudge and it has less than half the calories!

The secret to no-fat cooking is to provide food that looks, feels and tastes as good or better than fat-filled cooking. Too often I hear people object that no-fat cooking can't be as satisfying as the real thing. In the first place, no-fat cooking IS the real thing: it contains healthful, natural foods prepared in an intelligent fashion. I'd argue that it's fat-filled cooking that is NOT the real thing: it's loaded with added fat, added sugar, added salt and if store-bought, who knows how many artificial additives and preservatives? In the second place, I can prove that no-fat cooking is every bit as mouth-watering and satisfying as any mega-calorie fat-filled recipe. The proof is in your hands right now: try the no-fat fudge recipes in this book and you'll never go back to fatty fudges again. And in the third place, no-fat cooking is not just good eating, it's a great deal of fun, too.

We all rely on preset mental programs to tell us whether any food, no-fat or otherwise, is desirable. Failing any of four sensory tests will at best leave you disappointed and unsatisfied, and at worst send you running to the nearest bakery. If I offer you a plate and say, "Here, have some fudge", you would first examine what I offer you. Does it look like fudge? If it does, it's just passed the first of the four sensory tests. Next, you would probably pick up a piece, and unconsciously subject the fudge to the second sensory test: texture. Does it feel like fudge? If it does, you may go further and take a sniff or two of the fudge, giving it the third sensory test, smell.

If and only if you're satisfied with the results of the first three sensory tests, you'll move on to the final and most important test of all: Does it taste like fudge? If the answer is "yes", then you will accept what's in your mouth as "real" fudge and will look forward to another piece and perhaps a third.

For some time now I've been conducting classes on no-fat cooking. I'm proud that my techniques are proving popular and are gaining acceptance. I've founded the Kansas City No-Fat Culinary Institute, where others are being trained to teach no-fat cooking. If you've enjoyed my no-fat cookbooks, I encourage you to become an instructor. Inquiries should be addressed to:

DIET'S END
P.O. BOX 8009
SHAWNEE MISSION, KANSAS
66208

I hope you enjoy these fudges as much as I enjoyed developing them for you.

To your better health with just no fat!

Norman Rose ❖

YE OLDE FUDGE COMPANY
~ Original ~
No Fat Kanza Towne Est. 1994

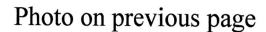

Photo on previous page

In this presentation I've matched an assortment of no fat fudges with the enchanting hybrid tea rose, Brigadoon, to illustrate the advantages of becoming lost occasionally.

Just as the main character in the hit Broadway play <u>Brigadoon,</u> became lost in the Scottish highlands and stumbled onto the mystical town of Brigadoon (Copyright 1954 by Loew's incorporated, renewed 1962 by Metro Goldwyn-Mayer Film Company, lyrics and music by Lerner and Loew) so too I became lost when trying to develop a butter flavored hot fudge sauce.

My no fat hot fudge sauce kept turning into a solid fudge-like mass!

And just as the main character in Brigadoon realized the magic he had encountered, I too understood the uniqueness of no fat fudge.

Imagine, America's favorite candy without the fat!

The Rose

Brigadoon, a 1992 All-America Rose winner creates enchantment you feel with every opening bloom. Long coral-pink buds open in graceful swirls then mature into exhibition blossoms with the coral-pink blending into a filigree of creamy lace. The color becomes vibrant as the blossom ages, heightening the bicolor effect. It is a vigorous and spectacular rose.

Photo On Page 4

That's Pumpkin Fudge in the silver box with Cherry-Berry Fudge to the right surrounded by assorted Bon Bons and Truffles and a small box of Peanut Butter-Chocolate Fudge.

The Roses are Orangeade, New Year and Tropicana.

Photo On Page 5

The Fudge is Coconut-Rum-Raisin and the whisky bottle is from the early 1800's.

The red roses are Olympiads, the multicolor roses are Anticipations and the white roses are John F. Kennedys.

INTRODUCTION TO NO-FAT FUDGE

Why bother with no-fat fudge?

No-fat cooking isn't just for diets and weight-loss schemes. There's more to it than just a healthful, satisfying lifestyle.

No-fat cooking simply tastes better than fat cooking.

Removing fat leaves more room for flavor. When properly prepared, no-fat foods consistently taste fresher and more flavorful than their fatty versions.

That may seem incredible at first. How can no-fat possibly be more flavorful? We've been led to believe all our lives that flavor and fat are inseparable, that all the flavor is in the fat. Once and for all let's dispel that myth!

Pure fat is tasteless, odorless and adds NO flavor to food.

Have you ever heard of anyone sneaking into the kitchen and secretly eating half a can of shortening? When was the last time you eagerly chug-a-lugged half a bottle of soybean oil? Never? Why not?

Because there is no flavor, that's why! When fat is removed from our food nothing is lost when it comes to flavor. Sometimes texture may be involved, but never flavor.

Let me confess outright, it's true that few if any foods are 100% free of fat. Technology just does not exist yet to eliminate it entirely. But we can remove enough fat from our food to make what's left over virtually insignificant. By US government standards, any food item with a per-serving fat content less than 0.5 gram may be properly called "fat free",

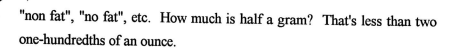

"non fat", "no fat", etc. How much is half a gram? That's less than two one-hundredths of an ounce.

Let's consider the fat content of the ingredients of both regular peanut butter fudge and my no-fat Chunky No Peanut Butter Fudge.

THE FAT CONTENT OF PEANUT BUTTER FUDGE
(In grams of fat)

	Regular (24 servings)	No Fat (24 servings)
1 cup evaporated milk whole vs skim	19	1
3 tablespoons butter vs. butter sprinkles	33	0
1 cup peanuts vs garbanzos	71	4
Fat from sugar	0	0
Total grams of fat	123	5
Total calories from fat	1107	45

With each gram of fat bringing 9 calories to the table it is easy to see that by removing the fat we also remove an enormous number of calories.

In this example, our batch of peanut butter fudge is 1,062 calories lighter without the fat. When cut into 24 pieces, each serving of regular fudge has over 5 grams of fat and over 46 calories from fat. Each serving of our no-fat fudge has only 2 calories from fat and contains only 0.2 grams of fat. You've just succeeded in removing 44 calories and 4.8 grams of fat from each piece, without sacrificing taste.

This recipe comes in well beneath the government standard for "No fat." The recipe is delicious as it is, but you can afford to garnish it with real peanuts and still stay within the no-fat standard. This recipe could have more than twice as much fat and still meet the government standard. Only if fat content increased to 12 grams in the entire recipe would our fudge be considered fat (12 grams/24 pieces = 0.5 grams of fat per serving).

So let's sprinkle on top of our fudge one tablespoon of chopped peanuts. This will add about 5 grams of fat, bringing our total fat content to 10 grams and our per-serving content to 0.41 grams. Even with this indulgence, our recipe is well within the 0.5 gram definition of no-fat. The chopped peanuts add a dramatic visual message and that message is:

This is unquestionably peanut butter fudge!

The garbanzos (also called chick peas-- see page 25) give the fudge the same texture as regular peanut butter fudge.

To complete the effect, I like to add a little artificial peanut butter flavoring to the recipe. My personal favorite is made by a company called Watkins[R]. It's the most delicious, outrageous peanut butter flavor I've ever encountered. I recommend you look these folks up in your local telephone book and obtain some of this product.

All the fudge recipes in this book contain less than 12 grams of fat (0.5 grams per serving), and therefore are properly called "no fat" fudges. Some of the recipes herein have as little as one gram of fat for the entire batch (about 0.04 grams per serving).

NO-FAT FUDGE IS AS EASY AS 1-2-3

Fat-free fudge is fun to make. Forget about candy thermometers, soft balls, ice cubes, lots of steps, etc. And especially forget about beating your candy until you are blue in the face. All you'll need to remember are three basic steps for each recipe:

     1. Combine initial ingredients
     2. Boil and stir for 5 minutes or less
     3. Add final ingredients and cool properly

Fudge has never been as easy as this.

Humidity doesn't hurt these fudges, so feel free to make some on a rainy, dreary day. It'll give you two reasons to pick up your spirits: it'll give you something fun to do and give you something fun to eat as well.

WHAT IS FUDGE?

Any fudge, no-fat or otherwise, is nothing more than sugar that has been liquefied by boiling and then enticed to become crystalline while in a moist environment. Butter and milk flavors are always included while other flavors can be added. When the sugar crystals formed are small, your fudge will be fine-grained. When appropriate moisture is retained, your fudge will be creamy. Note: by 'creamy' I mean creamy. Don't confuse 'creamy' with the greasy feel you get from store-bought fudges that use butter flavored partially hydrogenated vegetable oil.

The no-fat fudge recipes in this book fall basically in two categories: marshmallow fudges and old-fashioned sugared fudges. The two types will require somewhat different techniques, but are both great fun to make:

NO-FAT MARSHMALLOW FUDGES

These fudge recipes rely upon miniature marshmallows for several important functions in the fudge-making process.

Marshmallows provide a necessary 'shock' to the hot candy mixture as they are poured into the hot skillet. The liquid sugar mixture immediately starts trying to return to a crystalline form as it is suddenly cooled down. But it can't crystallize completely just yet because it is still too hot and because it has been surrounded by a sea of sticky marshmallow. Once the marshmallows have been thoroughly mixed and totally dissolved, the hot candy is poured into a plate or platter. Now it can seriously begin its cooling and 'fudging' process.

As the candy cools, it 'fudges,' first in the center of the plate, and then gradually working its way to the outer edges. The marshmallows provide body, substance, and texture to the fudge. Because the fudging process spreads outward slowly, you have time to work with the fudge to give it any desired finishing touches.

The sticky nature of the marshmallows allows you to put a beautiful filigree finish (page 106) on your fudge, if desired. This technique is not possible with regular sugared fudges.

Marshmallow fudges go through several stages of consistency on its way to completion. They change from a hot boiling liquid to a sticky taffy, to a tacky caramel, and finally to a firm fudge. The amount of time required to become firm is determined by the amount of moisture in the fudge. To reduce the setup time, reduce the amount of liquid in your recipe or increase the boiling time. (Or maybe a little of both.)

These marshmallow fudges have a texture adored by some fudge lovers. It is much firmer, like store-bought candy bar fudge, and doesn't dissolve in your mouth as fast as our Old-Fashioned Sugared Fudges.

Leftovers made by this recipe hold their texture better than regular fudge when wrapped in plastic and stored. The original fresh, warm, gourmet feel to this fudge can be easily restored by microwaving just before serving. I usually place two pieces on a saucer and microwave on high for 10 seconds. Just be careful not to melt it.

NO-FAT OLD-FASHIONED SUGARED FUDGES

These are fudges like grandma used to make when she had a good day and a lot of luck. Odds are though that she never even thought of making

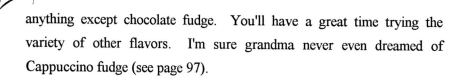

anything except chocolate fudge. You'll have a great time trying the variety of other flavors. I'm sure grandma never even dreamed of Cappuccino fudge (see page 97).

The method required here calls for you to pour the hot candy onto a sheet pan that is sitting on top of a wet, cold dish towel. The temperature shock initiates the "fudging" process. As you move the candy around with a stiff spatula or other tool, you can actually feel the consistency changing in a few places, on the bottom, as the mixture begins to crystallize. Mix these developing crystals throughout your mixture to promote a faster, more uniform fudging action. This mixing will make your fudge creamier and more delightful. This sounds more complicated than it is.

CONCLUSION

If you want a fudge like the fudge from the your favorite fudge shop then you should concentrate on the Olde Fashioned Sugared Fudges. You can't wrap these fudges in plastic and keep them for a long time, but then they are so good that you won't want to store them. These fudges are easy to cut and are soft and creamy.

If a firm fudge is your desire then the Marshmallow Fudges are your best bet. You can wrap these fudges in plastic and they will keep for a long, long time. They are excellent for lunch box treats. I have stored these fudges at room temperature for months at a time.

In order to obtain a true butter flavor you will note that each recipe calls for "All natural butter-flavored sprinkles." I have successfully used both Molly McButter(R), All Natural Dairy Sprinkles (Natural Butter Flavor) and All Natural, Butter Buds(R) Brand, Butter Flavored Mix.❖

BASIC INSTRUCTIONS

Throughout the past one hundred years, thousands of fudge recipes have been written. In the beginning things were fairly simple. Part of the delight of fudge was how simple it all was. But now fudge recipes and directions have become so long, detailed, and complicated as to scare off many fudge lovers from even trying to make this traditional American candy.

The no-fat fudges in this book are a snap to prepare. They will result in a perfect fudge almost every time. In fact, the marshmallow fudge recipes in this book will ALWAYS turn to fudge successfully if you let them sit long enough.

EQUIPMENT

If you have my third cookbook, Favorite Foods - No Fat Cooking (published by WRS Publishing, Waco, Texas, 1994) you should have acquired a 10 inch cast iron skillet, a 10 inch cast iron Dutch oven (approximately 4 quart) and a stainless steel whisk. The marshmallow fudges require an electric hand mixer, not to beat the fudge, but rather to thoroughly mix in the marshmallows as they are melting.

The old-fashioned sugared fudges require a sheet pan approximately 11 inches by 17 inches by 1 inch deep in which to cool, 'fudge,' and cream the candy. For these fudges you will also need a tool to move and scrape the bottom of the sheet pan to promote an even-grained fudging process. This tool can be a stiff, rigid spatula, a plastic pastry scraper, a pancake turner, or even (I'm not kidding) a car windshield ice scraper. The ice scraper is just about ideal for this kind of work. Of course, you should use a new, unused ice scraper which you will clean and store just like any other kitchen tool. I won't guarantee results if you use an old ice scraper from your glove compartment. (I'd hate to have bugs get to my fudge before I do.)

OLD-FASHIONED SUGARED FUDGES

Recipes will ask you to measure and mix initial ingredients in a 10- inch cast iron Dutch oven. If you have an electric stove, preheat the largest burner to the highest temperature. Gas stoves do not need to be preheated.

Use aluminum foil to line a casserole dish or pan that is approximately 6 inches by 9 inches by 2 inches deep. There is no need to spray or grease the pan because these recipes will not stick.

Moisten two dish towels thoroughly with cold tap water, wring out excess water and spread singly on countertop. These will be needed to rapidly cool the mixture and start the 'fudging' process. Place a sheet pan that is approximately 11 inches by 17 inches by 1 inch deep on one of the cold, wet towels. Place a scraper or spatula nearby.

Place the cast iron Dutch oven containing your ingredients onto the preheated burner and stir continuously. When the mixture comes to a full rolling boil, set an accurate timer to the time called for in the recipe. When boiling is completed, remove the Dutch oven from the hot burner and continue stirring until the mixture stops boiling.

Add any remaining ingredients called for and mix well.

Pour mixture onto the sheet pan. Be very careful! This mixture is extremely hot and sticky. If you touch it, it will burn the thunder out of you and be difficult to remove. Please make sure no children are close by during this phase of your fudge making.

Spread mixture evenly and allow to cool for two or three minutes.

Using a scraper or stiff spatula, move candy mixture around . It is crucial to mix the candy that is starting to crystallize (make fudge), with the candy that is not crystallizing. This 'fudging' action will begin on the bottom of the pan where it is cold, so it is essential to scrape the bottom of the sheet pan and combine the 'fudging' crystals with the rest of the candy.

After the candy has cooled on the first wet towel for three or four minutes, move the sheet pan to the second cold, wet towel and continue to scrape and mix. Take the first towel, which has undoubtedly become very warm, and place it under a cold stream of tap water until it is cold again. Place it on the countertop. Repeat this process as long as necessary to assure that there is a cold, wet towel under the pan at all times. (An option is to use one long towel that is two or three times longer than your sheet pan and just move the sheet pan to a cold part of the towel as one part heats up under the hot sheet pan.)

Stay alert! When the mixture appears to be thickening evenly, it is time to pour it into the foil lined pan. As the mixture cools and thickens, begin moving and accumulating the mass of candy towards the corner from which you are going to pour it into the foil lined pan. You must pour while the mixture is still a thick liquid and before it solidifies.

Use a tablespoon to spread mixture evenly and to remove any air bubbles. Apply any desired toppings before fudge has set. Decorative swirls can be applied as fudge is firming. After fudge is firm, remove fudge with aluminum foil in place, peel the foil from the sides of fudge and cut into portions. Place pieces of fudge onto a plate or platter that has been sprinkled lightly with chopped nut meats or coarse cornflake crumbs. This will allow air to circulate on the bottom of the fudge, thereby allowing a crust to form on all sides and ensuring a stable fudge. An alternate method allowing the bottom to 'crust-up' would be to remove the fudge from the aluminum foil and place the fudge upside down with the bottom exposed to the air, thereby letting a very thin crust form on the bottom. This latter method is the one that I use on a regular basis. If you

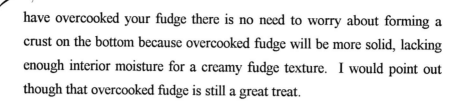

have overcooked your fudge there is no need to worry about forming a crust on the bottom because overcooked fudge will be more solid, lacking enough interior moisture for a creamy fudge texture. I would point out though that overcooked fudge is still a great treat.

Do **not** wrap this fudge in plastic or store in an airtight container.

MARSHMALLOW FUDGES

Assemble, measure and place ingredients to be cooked in a 10 inch cast iron skillet or a 10 inch cast iron Dutch oven, if called for. Place your stainless steel whisk next to the stove and preheat the largest burner on an electric stove by turning burner temperature control to the highest setting. (If using a gas stove there is no need to preheat the burner.)

Before we begin cooking the candy, prepare these other items:

Prepare a plate or platter by spraying it with a butter-flavored vegetable spray and set it on a wire cooling rack.

Next, measure out marshmallows and set them in front of the electric hand mixer. You will also need several tablespoons, so get them out and have them close by.

Place mixture on the preheated burner. Mix and stir continuously!

When mixture comes to a full rolling boil, set an accurate timer and continue stirring.

When boiling time is completed, remove mixture from heat and continue stirring until liquid stops boiling.

Add marshmallows and combine using a tablespoon to mix the hot batter. Eventually you can mix with a hand mixer, but at first you must use a spoon until the mixture is somewhat thinned. If you use a hand mixer too early the hot marshmallow will climb up the beaters and won't come down. Mix until smooth and the marshmallows are thoroughly melted (About a minute or so).

If called for, add any additional ingredients, mix well and pour mixture out onto the veggie-sprayed plate or platter and place it on the wire cooling rack.

Air bubbles will rise to the surface. Take a tablespoon and remove them by gently swirling the top of the candy. Check your candy every few minutes by swirling the top with a tablespoon. When swirls begin to hold their shape, it is time to apply your final pattern or design to the top of the fudge.

The fudge will first become firm in the center gradually working its way out to the edges. As soon as the fudge has firmed up in the center, use a butter knife to raise and shape the outer edges.

When the fudge has completely set, use a thin-bladed knife to score and cut the fudge. Cover with plastic wrap and store (provided there is anything left after you have finished sampling this delicious fudge).

If pieces are individually wrapped in plastic, they will keep for a long, long time. (This fudge never spoils if properly eaten.)

CRITIQUING YOUR FIRST FUDGE AND MAKING ADJUSTMENTS

These fudges rely solely upon moisture for their creamy texture. When properly prepared, they will exceed every expectation of what a great fudge should be.

It is not difficult to prepare great fudge!

Since the amount of moisture remaining in the finished fudge is critical, seven factors must be considered:

First, make sure that you accurately measure ingredients.

Second, be sure to use the equipment that is called for in the recipe. Either a 10 inch cast iron skillet or a 10 inch cast iron Dutch oven is called for in every recipe. These are essential to achieving consistent results. Cast iron skillets and Dutch ovens are available at most large discount stores and are reasonably priced. They provide a more uniform delivery of heat to the candy as it cooks. I have NEVER burned a batch of fudge while using cast iron cookware. A cast iron Dutch oven concentrates the heat from the burner and will provide a more vigorous boil to the candy mixture than a similar-sized cast iron skillet. Don't use the skillet when the Dutch oven is called for, and likewise, don't use the Dutch oven if the recipe asks for a skillet.

Third, use an accurate, consistent timer in controlling boiling time. Adjustments can be made later, but until you become familiar with the recipes, adhere strictly to the boiling times called for in the recipe.

Fourth, YOU must decide what a 'full rolling boil' is, as called for in every recipe. Be consistent in what you call a 'full rolling boil.' Give the mixture a little time to come to a general boil before setting the timer. That is, start the timer at the same point of the boiling cycle every time.

Fifth, understand that the secret of this fudge is in maintaining the proper amount of moisture in the finished product. Your stove is probably different than mine. Your burner may be hotter or cooler than mine. Consequently, the amount of moisture boiled off during a timed cooking cycle will vary according to the intensity of the boil. For example, a simmering boil gives off less steam than a vigorous, full rolling boil and this steam is moisture leaving your fudge.

Sixth, if your fudge is too firm because you used the wrong equipment or your burner is real hot, don't give up. Next time reduce the amount of boiling time called for in the recipe by a half minute and continue to do this until you find the right boiling time for perfect fudge. An example:

The recipe calls for a 10 inch cast iron skillet and you decided to use a 10-inch copper-bottomed stainless steel skillet. The recipe calls for a timed boiling period of 5 minutes and your fudge, when finished, sets up too quickly and is too firm.

Corrective adjustment:

Reduce timed boiling period from 5 minutes to 4 1/2 minutes and if perfection is achieved, decrease the boiling time periods for all the recipes by 1/2 minute.

Seventh, if your fudge isn't firm enough and it takes a long time to set up, next time increase the boiling time called for in the recipe in 1/2 minute increments until you achieve perfection, then note the boiling time difference and adapt this cooking time difference to all the other recipes. An example:

The recipe calls for a 10 inch cast iron Dutch oven and you use a four quart copper-clad stainless steel Dutch oven. The recipe calls for a timed boiling period of 4 1/2 minutes and your fudge, when finished, is not firm enough.

Corrective adjustment:

Increase the boiling time period to 5 minutes for your next try and if perfection is achieved, increase the boiling time periods for all the other recipes by 1/2 minute.

In summary:

--Use the proper equipment.

--Be consistent.

--Be prepared to change the cooking times called for in the recipes if you are not instantly successful.

Follow these guidelines and you will be successful, I guarantee it. ❖

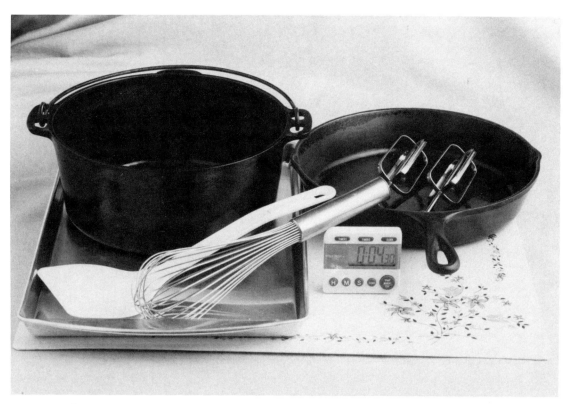

Necessary equipment: On the left is a 10 inch cast iron Dutch Oven with a sheet pan and scraper used in making the Olde Fashioned Sugared Fudges. On the right is a 10 inch cast iron skillet and blades for an electric mixer used with the Marshmallow Fudges. Both fudges require the use of the wire whisk and the accurate timer.

'NUT' MEATS AND OTHER CRUNCHIES

God bless garbanzos!

Garbanzo beans, also known as chick peas, are the ideal no-fat nut substitute. They look like nuts, chop up like nuts, and when properly used in your recipe, will satisfy even the hard-core nut lover. Garbanzos have very little taste of their own, so I recommend sprinkling a small quantity of the real nut over the top of your fudge. This will give you the taste of nuts, the look of nuts, and virtually no fat.

Never use more than one tablespoon of real nuts per batch, and only then as a topping. Even this small amount used to garnish the top of fudge will convince your subconscious that all the 'crunch' in the fudge comes from real nuts, when it's really from garbanzos. One tablespoon of peanuts contains about 5 grams of fat while pecans and walnuts will contain from 6 to 8 grams of fat. For example, the holiday Fruit Cake fudge on page 57 is topped with just 1 tablespoon of chopped pecans. Your brain will tell you there are pecans all through the fudge. But inside is a cup of garbanzos, not pecans. This is delightfully deceitful to the tastebuds.

Purchase dried chick peas for all no-fat recipes. They can be found in most supermarkets alongside dried beans, or sometimes in the Mexican food section. DO NOT use canned chick peas because they won't give you the crunchy texture you're looking for, and unlike the dried variety they have an unusual, undesirable flavor.

To prepare your chick peas, rinse them, cover with water, and allow to soak overnight. The following day, boil garbanzos for one hour and 15 minutes, drain thoroughly and use immediately or store in the refrigerator. When refrigerated they will keep like any other similar food. The exception to this procedure is the recipe for German Chocolate Fudge on page 89. Here, the boiling time is reduced to just 15 minutes because a crispier, crunchy texture is desired. This procedure adds significantly to the perceived texture of the 'pecans' and 'coconut' in this spectacular fudge.

No-fat fudges rely solely upon water or moisture for their 'creamy' texture. Garbanzos absorb a lot of water during preparation and then slowly release their moisture. The moisture inside the garbonzos is crucial to the consistency of 'nut' fudges.

Chopping your garbanzos will reduce the risk of moisture problems. When whole garbanzos are used, tiny puddles of water will form around them. What actually happens is that sugar pulls out water from garbanzos about the same way that sugar removes water in a curing ham. Chopping garbanzos reduces the effect. I find that when chopped into eight pieces, garbanzos resemble real chopped nuts in both appearance and texture. When finely chopped in a food processor garbanzos become the consistency of peanut butter. Experiment with garbanzos to find the consistency you prefer.

USING BREAKFAST CEREALS

Some breakfast cereals work very well in creating desirable, crunchy textures in fudges and some do not. I haven't tried them all, so just because I don't mention a particular kind of cereal doesn't necessarily mean it won't work. Low fat granolas and branolas generally yield good results. But be careful if you experiment: carefully watch the fat content of any cereal you use. Remember that you want to keep the total fat content of your batch of fudge below 12 grams, or you'll be defeating your purpose.

Many of my recipes will recommend a cereal. The Coconut Macaroon Fudge on page 125 uses oat bran flakes to create a proper texture. Corn flakes won't work. They quickly become waterlogged and chewy. The Banana, Cream and Crunch Fudge on page 113 uses Post[(R)] Banana

Crunch (R) cereal for the best crunch. I use a low fat granola in the Maple Butter Nut Crunch Fudge recipe on page 117. And for the Chocolate Coconut Crunch Fudge on page 44 I use Post(R) Bran'nola(TM) Low Fat - Bran Granola Cereal. In this recipe, this cereal gives you a real comforting crunch on the first day and acts like coconut on the second day. All in all, it makes for a spectacular fudge. ❖

Garbonzos: On the bottom are dry, uncooked garbonzos. Clockwise are garbonzos after boiling and after chopping in a food processor.

CREATING YOUR OWN
SIGNATURE FUDGE

The no-fat fudge experience does not stop with the last recipe in this book! After you become familiar with the no-fat fudge techniques, I encourage you to experiment with fudge. Push the limits of your imagination. Create your very own fudge: a unique blending of your favorite flavors and textures, styled and finished with your distinctive artistic flair.

In this chapter I hope to stir up your adventurous spirit and plant a few seeds of imagination. After that, it's all up to you: let your imagination go to work to create a true masterpiece.

A basic tip: I recommend putting those imaginative, creative juices to work right after a brisk morning walk. Late night creations often turn out to be strange and bizarre when beheld by the light of the next day! (If strange and bizarre is what you're looking for, then go right ahead.)

Most variations will involve playing with the liquid ingredients of fudge. How you substitute liquids for one another will determine much of your success or failure. Remember, moisture is the crucial factor in getting your fudge to set up with the right consistency.

Another warning: make certain that any ingredients you substitute are no-fat, or you could accidently sabotage your intent to make truly no-fat fudge.

CREATING NEW MARSHMALLOW FUDGES

Let's look at the liquid ingredients in the Very Vanilla Fudge from page 49:

This recipe relies on 1/2 cup of milk plus 2 tablespoons to provide the moist, creamy texture expected in a fudge. What happens if you tinker with these liquids?

Suppose your creative juices and personal cravings lead you toward a strawberry fudge. Let's change our liquid to the following:

1/4 cup evaporated skim milk

1/4 cup strawberry jam

1   teaspoon strawberry flavoring

2   tablespoons water

To further modify this vanilla fudge recipe if you wanted to maintain the amount of milk solids in the original fudge, just add 1 tablespoon of non fat powdered milk. If your new creation sets up too quickly and becomes too firm, then try again using a little more skim milk or other liquid.

By "other liquid" I'm really opening the door to endless possibilities. Some alternate liquid sources you try might be:

* Frozen strawberry daiquiri mix
* Fresh cooked strawberries
* Sour cream (non fat of course)
* Buttermilk
* ANYTHING! Use your imagination

Experiment with any flavoring you can think of.

Another example:

Let's start with the Maple Butter Nut Crunch Fudge on page 117. Perhaps you really enjoy this combination of flavors but you find the fudge too sweet for your taste. In order to make it less sweet you might simply replace the 1/4 cup of maple syrup with a less sweet alternative. You might try substituting the same amount of water and adding some maple flavoring.

Or, leave the sweetened granola out of the recipe and substitute some not-as-sweet bran flakes cereal to the recipe to create a less sweet, more wholesome fudge.

I hope you're getting the urge to experiment a little. If you get as excited about the possibilities as I do, you'll feel like you've become a mad scientist.

Like any mad scientist, experimentation will result in a few failures from time to time, but don't let that stop you. Some experimental fudge will set up too quickly and be too firm. If this happens, try heating it for a few seconds in the microwave to bring back that original warm, creamy texture of freshly made fudge. Remember, even that other mad scientist, Dr. Frankenstein, needed to zap his experiment to make it come back to life.

Other times your fudge may not "fudge" at all but remain in the "taffy" or "caramel" stage. This will be especially true if you try to create fudge from citrus, like lemon or lime, or other highly acidic ingredients. The acid in the fresh juice often kills the fudging process in marshmallow fudges and you generally end up with "taffy." If you haven't used too much liquid, this "taffy" effort will eventually turn into fudge if allowed to sit out where the excess moisture can evaporate. I'll have you know that an experiment I conducted using pine-nut flavoring turned out too soft, but eventually converted to a good solid fudge after sitting around for four days! If you'd rather not wait for your creation to turn to fudge, why not just call it no-fat taffy, cut and wrap in plastic, and no one will be the wiser.

THE OLDE FASHIONED SUGARED FUDGES

The same approach outlined for marshmallow fudges can be used in substituting liquids and flavors in the olde fashioned sugared fudges. One caution however: if you replace a pure liquid like water or skimmed milk with a pureed fruit, you should reduce the total boiling time. Pureed fruit actually reduces the amount of liquid in your recipe and replaces it with fruit solids (pulp). Fruit substitutions will work fine as long as you are careful not not to boil away the liquid needed to ensure a creamy texture in your finished fudge.

For example, you might decide to alter a basic chocolate fudge, which originally asks for one cup plus 2 tablespoons of water. You decide to substitute one cup of pureed red raspberries (seeds removed) plus 2 tablespoons water. You will need to reduce the boiling time to 4 minutes to end up with a perfect chocolate-raspberry fudge. If your fudge sets up too fast and is too hard, next time add another tablespoon of water. Just remember, finding the proper amount of moisture is the key to making new fudges.

The possibilities are absolutely endless. Will they all work? I don't know, but the human brain can conquer just about any problem with sufficient determination. I'll leave the experimenting up to you. One question I haven't been able to answer is if non-fat sour cream can be used as a valid, workable ingredient in no-fat fudge. If one of you intrepid fudge pioneers finds out that it is, please drop me a line and let me know. ❖

For Little Hands

Here's a no-fat fudge recipe that your little ones can safely shape and mold almost like modelling clay. They can make toys they can eat! I recommend molding this fudge into little elf-like creatures I call "Fudgkins."

The Tale of the Fudgkins

Once upon a time in the fudge land of Neverwas, dwelt a colony of Fudgkins. Fudgkins are creatures made entirely out of fudge and only come to life when allowed to do so by the living imagination of a young person.

Through unanimous agreement, it was decreed that no Fudgkin should ever get any older than the age of four. Certainly many Fudgkins have been around for centuries, but once they reach the age of four, they stay at that age the rest of their lives, in a state of perpetual amazement and innocence.

At one time Fudgkins got older like everyone else. At the age of four, the weight of responsibility was not heavy and it was still all right, even expected, to pretend. At four it was still okay to sit on the driveway in October, piling leaves with a stick and talking to each leaf and to

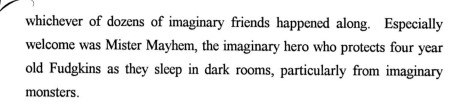

whichever of dozens of imaginary friends happened along. Especially welcome was Mister Mayhem, the imaginary hero who protects four year old Fudgkins as they sleep in dark rooms, particularly from imaginary monsters.

But Fudgkins who got older than four were ridiculed if they continued to pretend. By the time Fudgkins turned ten years old, they had lost their ability to pretend and had given up their make-believe friends, protectors and heroes, including Mister Mayhem. At the age of ten, Fudgkins started losing the ability to have fun and enjoy life.

The teenage years for Fudgkins proved to be particularly difficult. Teenage Fudgkins had lost the ability to make believe, and therefore bitterly made fun of young Fudgkins who still had imaginary friends. Older Fudgkins found teenage Fudgkins even harder to get along with. Old Fudgkins became very wise, but still were unable to have fun anymore.

At last a wise old Fudgkin with keen insight and knowledge put forward a proposal to limit the age of all Fudgkins to four years of age, so that all Fudgkins could have fun with imaginary friends forever. Teenage Fudgkins resisted the proposal, but in the end, they were easily outvoted and everybody went back to the age of four. That is precisely why you never see a Fudgkin over the age of four these days. ❖

Rules of the Kitchen
for
Little Hands
&
Mommies
When Making Fudgkins

Rule 1. Always wash your hands with soap and water.

Rule 2. Only Mommies are allowed to cook the fudge on page 39.

Rule 3. Only Mommies are allowed to melt pieces of fudge in the microwave.

Rule 4. **Mommies must make sure that melted fudge is cool and safe.**

Rule 5. "Little Hands" must always form the warm "Caramels" into Fudgkins.

Rule 6. Fudgkins are allowed to go to Pre-School for purposes of "Show & Tell".

Rule 7. Some Fudgkins should always be given or sent to Grandmas and Grandpas. ❖

Little Hands Chocolate Fudge

One of the beautiful properties of this fudge recipe is that after it has set up and cooled off it can be reheated in a microwave and it will revert back to a soft-caramel consistency. With this warm caramel, the little hands of your children (I like to call them "Little Hands") can shape and form their very own Fudgkins.

To create a nice warm caramel consistency, just place several pieces of this fudge in a microwave-approved cup or dish and microwave on high for 25 seconds or until fudge is just melted. DO NOT BOIL!

Allow melted fudge to cool by pouring it out onto a vegetable oil-sprayed plate and you'll find that the candy lingers for hours in a malleable, caramel stage. During this "caramel" stage, the candy can be easily sculpted and molded by Little Hands into free-form Fudgkins, provided an active imagination is at work. You will want to apply a little vegetable oil to your Little Hands so the caramel won't stick.

If you prefer, this fudge can be shaped in candy molds obtainable from your local hobby or crafts store. After washing molds, spray them with a butter-flavored vegetable oil spray. Little Hands should now be able to take the warm "Caramel" candy and press it into the molds.

Overnight, the soft caramel candy will cool and revert back to fudge. Then it's time for your children to play with, and snack upon, their new imaginary Fudgkin friends. ❖

LITTLE HANDS CHOCOLATE FUDGE

1   3.4 Ounce package JELL-O(R) Brand chocolate cook and serve pudding mix
11/2   Cups granulated sugar
2   Tablespoons all natural butter-flavored sprinkles
1/2   Cup plus 2 Tablespoons evaporated skimmed milk
5   Cups miniature marshmallows

Except for the marshmallows, place ingredients in a 10" cast iron skillet. Place your stainless steel whisk next to the stove. Before we begin cooking the candy, let's prepare some other items.

Prepare a plate or platter by spraying it with butter flavored vegetable spray and set it on a wire cooling rack. Next, measure the marshmallows and set them in front of the hand mixer. You'll need several tablespoons so get them out and have them handy.

Ok, let's start cooking. Place skillet on a large electric burner which is set to the hottest temperature. If using a gas stove, turn it to full on. Mix and stir continously.

When mixture comes to a full rolling boil, set an accurate timer to 5 minutes and continue stirring.

After 5 minutes, remove the skillet from the hot burner and continue stirring until mixture no longer boils.

Add marshmallows and combine using a tablespoon to mix marshmallows and the hot mixture. You can't use the hand mixer at first because the melting marshmallows will climb up the beaters and refuse to come down. By using a tablespoon first the mixture is somewhat thinned and now you can use the hand mixer effectively. Mix until smooth and the marshmallows are melted. (About a minute or so)

Pour mixture out onto the veggie sprayed plate or platter and place it on a wire rack to cool.

Check your candy every few minutes by swirling the top. Shortly, (usually within 10 to 30 minutes) these swirls will begin to hold their shape. Apply your final pattern or design.

Use a butter knife to raise and shape the edges of your fudge. Remember, the outer edges will set up last.

When set, use a thin bladed knife to score or cut the fudge. Cover with plastic wrap. Some pieces of this fudge can be individually wrapped in plastic wrap and stored until it is needed by Little Hands in the production of Fudgkins. ❖

Fudge is one of the best mistakes an American ever made.

Who did it, we'll never know.

❀

BEGINNERS FUDGE
RECIPES

✿

Olde Fashioned Sugared Fudges

✿

Marshmallow Fudges

✿

This Vanilla fudge was selected as a beginners fudge because of its simplicity. With just four ingredients, there is not a lot to purchase and no worries about adding additional ingredients, during or after the cooking process.

All of your efforts and attention should be directed towards cooking the mixture for the correct number of minutes, stirring continously, cooling, creaming and then pouring the mixture into an aluminum foil-lined pan approximately 6" by 8" by 2".

You should assemble the following before commencing the cooking process:

> 10" cast iron Dutch oven
> Stainless steel wire whisk
> Aluminum foil-lined pan or dish, approximately 6" by 8" by 2"
> Sheet pan approximately 10" by 15"
> 2 cold wet towels
> An accurate timer

Put the cold wet towels on a counter top or table and place the sheet pan on one of them.

Before beginning please be sure to read the basic instructions beginning on page 17.

<u>**Crunchy Note**</u>:

For a **Butter Crunch Fudge**, after the 4 1/2 minute boiling period, add 1 teaspoon imitation butter flavoring, stir to mix and pour out into the sheet pan. Add 1 cup Post[(R)] Brand Bran'nola[(TM)] cereal and then continue with the recipe. This is a super, buttery-rich, crunchy fudge. ❖

VANILLA FUDGE

2 1/3 Cups granulated sugar
1   4.6 Oz. package JELL-O⁽ᴿ⁾ Brand Vanilla cook & serve pudding mix
3   Tablespoons all natural butter flavored sprinkles
1   Cup plus 2 tablespoons evaporated skimmed milk

If using an electric stove, preheat the largest burner to the highest heat prior to assembling ingredients in order to speed things up. Line a 6" by 8" by 2" pan or dish with aluminum foil. No need to veggie spray the foil.

Combine all ingredients in a 10 inch cast iron dutch oven. Place on preheated burner and bring to a full rolling boil while stirring continuously. Set an accurate timer for 4 1/2 minutes. (See note below). Continue to stir throughout the cooking process with a stainless steel whisk.

After boiling for the 4 1/2 minutes remove from heat and continue stirring until mixture stops boiling.

Set a sheet pan, approximately 10" by 15", on top of a cold wet towel (cold tap water is fine). Pour mixture onto the sheet pan. Using a plastic pastry scraper, spatula, or other flat utensil, move mixture around so as to combine and blend those fudge crystals beginning to form, in spots, on the bottom of the pan with the rest of the mixture.

After two or three minutes move sheet pan to a fresh cold towel and continue to scrape the fudging crystals from the bottom of the pan and to fold them into the mixture.

After a few minutes move pan to another cold towel and as mixture starts to thicken begin moving and accumulating the mixture to the corner of the pan from which you are going to pour mixture out into an aluminum foil lined pan approximately 6" by 8" by 2".

As mixture becomes very thick, pour out into the foil lined pan.

Using a tablespoon, spread fudge evenly throughout the pan. Swirl final design into the fudge.

When fudge is firm, lift the foil and fudge from the pan and cut the fudge into desired size pieces. Place pieces on plate or platter that has been sprinkled lightly with coarse corn flake pieces or chopped nut meats, thus allowing the bottoms to "crust" up along with the sides.

Note: Your cooking time may vary. See page 23. ❖

For the second beginners fudge I have chosen a classic.

This fudge is the fudge that has been prepared, over and over since fudge was first mistakenly created in some long forgotten American kitchen.

This is the fudge my mother made years ago when everything went perfectly. The difference being that this fudge has a finer-grained, smoother texture and no fat.

Generally, when I mention "fudge" to someone, they automatically think 'Chocolate fudge' and so for that reason, I have included this chocolate fudge. I'm sure you will agree that this fudge has very simple ingredients.

This is a great place to start!

Crunchy Note:

To make a Chocolate-Coconut Crunch Fudge, after the 4 1/2 minute boiling period add 1 teaspoon coconut extract, pour into the sheet pan then add 1 cup Post(R) Brand Bran'Nola(TM) cereal and continue with the recipe. As a topping for your fudge use 1 tablespoon of flaked coconut. This makes an outstanding fudge. ❖

NORMAN'S FAVORITE CHOCOLATE FUDGE

21/3 Cups granulated sugar
1   4.6 Oz. package JELL-O(R) Brand Vanilla cook & serve pudding mix
3   Tablespoons all natural butter flavored sprinkles
2   Tablespoons Dutch Processed European style cocoa
4   Tablespoons instant non fat dry milk powder
1   Cup plus 2 tablespoons water
1   Tablespoon pecan pieces

If using an electric stove, preheat the largest burner to the highest heat prior to assembling ingredients in order to speed things up. Line a 6" by 8" by 2" pan or dish with aluminum foil. No need to veggie spray the foil since the Olde Fashioned Sugared Fudges won't stick.

Except for the pecan pieces, combine all ingredients in a 10 inch cast iron dutch oven. Place on preheated burner and bring to a full rolling boil while stirring continuously. Set an accurate timer for 4 1/2 minutes. (See note below). Continue to stir throughout the cooking process with a stainless steel whisk.

After boiling for the 4 1/2 minutes remove from heat and continue stirring until mixture stops boiling.

Set a sheet pan, approximately 10" by 15", on top of a cold wet towel (cold tap water is fine). Pour mixture onto the sheet pan. Using a plastic pastry scraper, spatula, or other flat utensil, move mixture around so as to combine and blend those fudge crystals beginning to form, in spots, on the bottom of the pan with the rest of the mixture.

After two or three minutes move sheet pan to a fresh cold towel and continue to scrape the fudging crystals from the bottom of the pan and to fold them into the mixture.

After a few minutes move pan to another cold towel and as mixture starts to thicken begin moving and accumulating the mixture to the corner of the pan from which you are going to pour mixture out into an aluminum foil lined pan approximately 6" by 8" by 2".

As mixture becomes very thick, pour out into the foil lined pan.

Using a tablespoon, spread fudge evenly throughout the pan and sprinkle the pecan pieces on top. Swirl final design into the fudge.

When fudge is firm, lift the foil and fudge from the pan and cut the fudge into desired size pieces. Place pieces on plate or platter that has been sprinkled lightly with coarse corn flake pieces or chopped nut meats, thus allowing the bottoms to "crust" up along with the sides.

Note: Your cooking time may vary. See page 23. ❖

This marshmallow fudge recipe makes a nice after-dinner 'complemint' to your special meal.

For a peppermint flavor just use a peppermint extract.

After your fudge has set up it can be cut up into small pieces, melted in a microwave and poured into mint leaf candy molds that you can obtain from your local crafts store. ❖

Chocolate Mint Leaves

CHOCOLATE MINT

1   3.4 Ounce package JELL-O[(R)] Brand chocolate cook and serve pudding mix
11/2 Cups granulated sugar
1   Tablespoon all natural butter-flavored sprinkles
1/2 Cup plus 2 Tablespoons evaporated skimmed milk
1   Teaspoon mint extract
5   Cups miniature marshmallows

Except for the marshmallows, place ingredients in a 10" cast iron skillet. Place your stainless steel whisk next to the stove. Before we begin cooking the candy, let's prepare some other items.

Prepare a plate or platter by spraying it with butter flavored vegetable spray and set it on a wire cooling rack. Next, measure the marshmallows and set them in front of the hand mixer. You'll need several tablespoons so get them out and have them handy.

Ok, let's start cooking. Place skillet on a large electric burner which is set to the hottest temperature. If using a gas stove, turn it to full on. Mix and stir continously.

When mixture comes to a full rolling boil, set an accurate timer to 5 minutes and continue stirring.

After 5 minutes, remove the skillet from the hot burner and continue stirring until mixture no longer boils.

Add marshmallows and combine using a tablespoon to mix marshmallows and the hot mixture. You can't use the hand mixer at first because the melting marshmallows will climb up the beaters and refuse to come down. By using a tablespoon first the mixture is somewhat thinned and now you can use the hand mixer effectively. Mix until smooth and the marshmallows are melted. (About a minute or so)

Pour mixture out onto the veggie sprayed plate or platter and place it on a wire rack to cool.

Check your candy every few minutes by swirling the top. Shortly, (usually within 10 to 30 minutes) these swirls will begin to hold their shape. Apply your final pattern or design.

Use a butter knife to raise and shape the edges of your fudge. Remember, the outer edges will set up last.

When set, use a thin bladed knife to score or cut the fudge. Cover with plastic wrap and store what's left after you have appropriately sampled your fudge. ❖

This Very Vanilla marshmallow fudge, with its simple ingredients, is fun and easy to make and it never has failed me. If you do happen to undercook this fudge just let it sit about and it will turn into fudge.

Crunchy Note:

For a Vanilla-Granola fudge, as pictured below, just add a cup of low-fat granola after you have mixed-in and melted the marshmallows, then continue with instructions. ❖

Vanilla-Granola Fudge

VERY VANILLA FUDGE

1   3.0 Ounce package JELL-O^(R) Brand vanilla cook and serve pudding mix
11/2   Cups granulated sugar
1   Tablespoon all natural butter-flavored sprinkles
1/2   Cup plus 2 Tablespoons evaporated skimmed milk
5   Cups miniature marshmallows

Except for the marshmallows, place ingredients in a 10" cast iron skillet. Place your stainless steel whisk next to the stove. Before we begin cooking the candy, let's prepare some other items.

Prepare a plate or platter by spraying it with butter flavored vegetable spray and set it on a wire cooling rack. Next, measure the marshmallows and set them in front of the hand mixer. You'll need several tablespoons so get them out and have them handy.

Ok, let's start cooking. Place skillet on a large electric burner which is set to the hottest temperature. If using a gas stove, turn it to full on. Mix and stir continously.

When mixture comes to a full rolling boil, set an accurate timer to 5 minutes and continue stirring.

After 5 minutes, remove the skillet from the hot burner and continue stirring until mixture no longer boils.

Add marshmallows and combine using a tablespoon to mix marshmallows and the hot mixture. You can't use the hand mixer at first because the melting marshmallows will climb up the beaters and refuse to come down. By using a tablespoon first the mixture is somewhat thinned and now you can use the hand mixer effectively. Mix until smooth and the marshmallows are melted. (About a minute or so)

Pour mixture out onto the veggie sprayed plate or platter and place it on a wire rack to cool.

Check your candy every few minutes by swirling the top. Shortly, (usually within 10 to 30 minutes) these swirls will begin to hold their shape. Apply your final pattern or design.

Use a butter knife to raise and shape the edges of your fudge. Remember, the outer edges will set up last.

When set, use a thin bladed knife to score or cut the fudge. Cover with plastic wrap and store what's left after you have appropriately sampled your fudge. ❖

Above: On the left is a Lemon Butter Truffle Fudge center and on the right is a Chocolate Amaretto Truffle Fudge center. Both Are coated with the Double Dutch Chocolate Fudge from page 87.

HOLIDAY FUDGE, BON BONS
&
TRUFFLES

Bon is a french word meaning 'good', hence, bon bon translates into 'good good' and it is this 'goodness' which we seek in holiday candy making and the giving thereof.

A small box of hand made, fat-free holiday fudge, bon bons, or truffles, carefully wrapped and lovingly presented, is a gift well received. It is a gift of yourself, your time, your talent, and it is a powerful illustration of your concern for the health and well being of the recipient.

Your gift box could consist of a variety of fudges, which would be excellent, or it might be a wildly imaginative assortment of fudges, bon bons, and truffles containing many hand dipped fudges, creams, or fruit centers.

HOLIDAY FUDGE

The three holiday fudges I have included are intended to add a lot of color, uniqueness, flavor and excitement to your holiday dessert table. If you like fruit cake you'll love this Fruit Cake Fudge. If pumpkin pie is your forte then be sure to include the Pumpkin Fudge. Of course everyone loves the maraschino cherries and strawberries found in the Cherry-Berry Fudge. These fudges are not hard to prepare, just be sure to follow the instructions.

BON BONS

Let's consider the basic fudges available for making bon bon coatings. Only the Olde Fashioned Sugared Fudges should be used as coating fudges. The Marshmallow Fudges, when re-melted, are too sticky to use in this manner. The vanilla fudge found on page 43 can be used to make a wide assortment of flavored and colored coatings for the bon bons. As an example, place two or three pieces of this fudge along with 1/4 teaspoon lemon extract and a few drops of yellow food color in a microwave approved dish or cup (hereafter called a Fudge pot), and microwave on high until melted. (About 20 seconds in my microwave) Remove from microwave and stir to mix the color and flavor. You now have a lemon flavored, yellow colored coating mixture into which you might dip small cubes of other fudges or small marble-size pieces of the French Cream from page 65 or the Variety Creams from page 67. A pink raspberry coating goes well around a French Cream center. When flavored with almond extract and used to coat cubes of Fruit Cake Fudge from page 57, a really unique flavor combination is achieved.

The second fudge to consider should be a batch of Double Dutch Chocolate Fudge from page 87. With this fudge melted in your fudge pot you can chocolate coat almost anything. One of my favorites is to chocolate coat cubes of Chocolate Amaretto Truffle Fudge from page 77. Another favorite bon bon center is the Chunky No Peanut Butter Fudge from page 105. Of course the French Cream from page 65 and the Variety Creams from page 67 were designed expressly to be used as bon bon centers and for this purpose they will provide a lot of excitement and sighs of contentment.

FABRICATING THE BON BON

After you have selected and prepared a fudge to be used as the bon bon coating, you should next prepare a base on which a just-dipped center can be placed. This is accomplished by melting in the microwave a few pieces of your coating fudge in your fudge pot. [*The secret here is to melt the fudge but you DON'T want to BOIL the fudge. If you do boil the coating fudge in the microwave it tends to stick to the aluminum foil for a while. If you let it harden it will come free from the foil and will have a somewhat grainier texture, however it will still be good.*] Now, after the fudge is melted use a teaspoon to pour a small amount out onto an ungreased piece of aluminum foil. This will be the base of your bon bon and should be about the size of a quarter and about 1/16 inch thick. Pour out as many bases as you will need.

Next, refill your fudge pot with coating fudge and melt in the microwave.

If you are going to use the French Cream on page 65 or the Variety Creams on page 67 they should have been prepared in advance and allowed to chill for at least an hour in the freezer. Remove the creams from the freezer and using a teaspoon, spoon out enough of this course mixture to make a small marble. This mixture, on the second day, will be real firm and will tend to crumble somewhat. Not to worry though, just place a teaspoon of powdered sugar in the palm of your left hand and then put the piece or pieces of cream on top. Use your right hand and fingers to form the cream into the shape of a marble. The heat of your hands and the pressure of your fingers reforms the cream into a bon bon center that closely resembles a marble. The powdered sugar will keep the cream from sticking to your hands, but any excess powdered sugar remaining on the finished bon bon center should be removed by either pressing it into the bon bon center or rubbing it off of the bon bon center. Excess powdered sugar remaining on the center will complicate the dipping and coating process as the coating fudge does not like to stick to powdered sugar. Prepare as many bon bon centers as will be required.

Re-heat your fudge pot so that the coating fudge is melted. Drop a prepared bon bon center into the fudge pot, submerse to completely coat and quickly remove with a two prong fork. Draw the bottom of the fork across the top of the fudge pot to remove excess coating and place on a prepared base. If you leave the bon bon center in the hot fudge pot too long it will melt just like the fudge, so be quick about coating the bon bon centers.

If you want to use other fudges as bon bon centers select those fudges that you desire, being attentive to the fact that some of these fudges 'age' better than others. For instance the coconut macaroon fudge from page 125, is intended to be eaten within a couple of days, or so, since the bran flakes tend to become chewy as they absorb the internal moisture of the fudge. The Olde Fashioned Sugared Fudges become finer grained with age and should not be wrapped in plastic wrap or stored in air tight containers, whereas the marshmallow fudges store quit well in plastic wrap. Just cut the fudge that you have chosen to be used as centers for your bon bons into appropriate sized cubes, dip them briefly into your fudge pot and place them on a prepared base.

While your finished bon bons are still warm take a paring knife and trim the base of any excess. If you have messed up on some, just allow them to cool and then re-dip them.

By adding a teaspoon of finely chopped nuts to the fudge in your fudge pot you can create a very interesting and inviting texture to your bon bon coating.

TRUFFLES

Eating truffles has been described as the nearest thing to eating pure chocolate. I had always thought of a truffle as having a dark creamy chocolate center, covered with a dark chocolate snappy coating. Recently, much to my surprise, I discovered a large variety of truffles that were semi creamy tidbits of various flavors, rolled and dusted with ground nuts, coconut, or bitter cocoa. In other words, according to contemporary standards, a truffle is in the eye of the person marketing the candy. Feel free to do your own version of a truffle, as you understand it should be.

You should know that the Truffle Fudges, in this chapter, rely on an extra measure of moisture being retained in the finished fudge. This is accomplished by slightly undercooking the fudge.

These Truffle Fudges are so creamy that it seems as though they almost look for any excuse to lose their 'fudge' texture and revert back into a 'cream' texture. It is this characteristic that allows us to end up with a very creamy, smooth center for our Truffles.

For outstanding fudge Truffles, select any of the truffle fudges from page 71 through page 79. After the fudge has finally firmed up, cut into desired size pieces and chill in the freezer, then dip them in Double Dutch Chocolate Fudge and allow them to 'Crust' up. On the second day these truffle centers will have reverted back to a very creamy consistency and exactly mimic a regular fatty truffle center. In fact they will be better than most. With these little jewels it is important to allow air to circulate around the bottoms in order to accomplish a firm base. Occasionally turning a fresh truffle on its side during the 'crusting' process will aid in establishing a stable delicacy. ❖

HOLIDAY FUDGE RECIPES

✦

✦

That great entertainer, Johnny Carson, often remarked that there existed only one fruit cake in the whole world and people just shipped it around without ever eating it because no one liked it.

Well, I've met a lot of folks who do like to eat fruit cake and if you are one of them, then I know you'll love this fudge.

You will experience the chewy texture of candied fruit, the crunch of "nuts", the flavors of fruit & rum, all set against a backdrop of creamy butter-vanilla.

A unique and colorful addition to any holiday feast with less than a half gram of fat per serving.

FRUIT CAKE FUDGE

21/3   Cups granulated sugar
1   4.6 Oz. package JELL-O(R) Brand Vanilla cook & serve pudding mix
2   Tablespoons all natural butter flavored sprinkles
3/4   Cup evaporated skimmed milk
1   Cup "Nut Meats" (See page 25)
1/2   Cup candied fruit cake fruit, chopped
1/2   Teaspoon rum flavor
1   Teaspoon Watkins(R) Brand imitation mixed fruit extract
1/2   Tablespoon small pecan pieces

If using an electric stove, preheat the largest burner to the highest heat prior to assembling ingredients in order to speed things up. Line a 6" by 8" by 2" pan or dish with aluminum foil. No need to veggie spray the foil.

Except for the pecans, combine all ingredients in a 10 inch cast iron dutch oven. Place on preheated burner and bring to a full rolling boil while stirring continuously. Set an accurate timer for 4 1/2 minutes. (See note below). Continue to stir throughout the cooking process with a stainless steel whisk.

After boiling for the 4 1/2 minutes remove from heat and continue stirring until mixture stops boiling.

Set a sheet pan, approximately 10" by 15", on top of a cold wet towel (cold tap water is fine). Pour mixture onto the sheet pan. Using a plastic pastry scraper, spatula, or other flat utensil, move mixture around so as to combine and blend those fudge crystals beginning to form, in spots, on the bottom of the pan with the rest of the mixture.

After two or three minutes move sheet pan to a fresh cold towel and continue to scrape the fudging crystals from the bottom of the pan and to fold them into the mixture.

After a few minutes move pan to another cold towel and as mixture starts to thicken begin moving and accumulating the mixture to the corner of the pan from which you are going to pour mixture out into an aluminum foil lined pan approximately 6" by 8" by 2".

As mixture becomes very thick, pour out into the foil lined pan.

Using a tablespoon, spread fudge evenly throughout the pan and **sprinkle the pecan pieces on top** of fudge. Swirl final design into the fudge.

When fudge is firm, lift the foil and fudge from the pan and cut the fudge into desired size pieces. Place pieces on plate or platter that has been sprinkled lightly with coarse corn flake pieces or chopped nut meats, thus allowing the bottoms to "crust" up along with the sides.

Note: Your cooking time may vary. See page 23. ❖

This unusual fudge is a true holiday fudge. It is perfectly comfortable resting among other traditional dessert buffet goodies such as pies, cakes, and cookies. The gleeful expressions of folks tasting this Pumpkin fudge for the first time will long be remembered.

On a holiday feast day, after the main meal has been consumed and an appropriate amount of time has passed, a piece of this fudge will add an exclamation point to the days gastronomical activities.

An added benefit, of course, is the fact that each piece contains only a trace of fat.

PUMPKIN FUDGE

21/3   Cups granulated sugar
1   4.6 Oz. package JELL-O(R) Brand Vanilla cook & serve pudding mix
2   Tablespoons all natural butter flavored sprinkles
1/2   Cup canned pumpkin
1/2   Teaspoon pumpkin pie spice
1/2   Cup plus 2 tablespoons evaporated skimmed milk
1   Tablespoon pecan pieces

If using an electric stove, preheat the largest burner to the highest heat prior to assembling ingredients in order to speed things up. Line a 6" by 8" by 2" pan or dish with aluminum foil. No need to veggie spray the foil.

Except for the pecan pieces, combine all ingredients in a 10 inch cast iron dutch oven. Place on preheated burner and bring to a full rolling boil while stirring continuously. Set an accurate timer for 4 1/2 minutes. (See note below). Continue to stir throughout the cooking process with a stainless steel whisk.

After boiling for the 4 1/2 minutes remove from heat and continue stirring until mixture stops boiling.

Set a sheet pan, approximately 10" by 15", on top of a cold wet towel (cold tap water is fine). Pour mixture onto the sheet pan. Using a plastic pastry scraper, spatula, or other flat utensil, move mixture around so as to combine and blend those fudge crystals beginning to form, in spots, on the bottom of the pan with the rest of the mixture.

After two or three minutes move sheet pan to a fresh cold towel and continue to scrape the fudging crystals from the bottom of the pan and to fold them into the mixture.

After a few minutes move pan to another cold towel and as mixture starts to thicken begin moving and accumulating the mixture to the corner of the pan from which you are going to pour mixture out into an aluminum foil lined pan approximately 6" by 8" by 2".

As mixture becomes very thick, pour out into the foil lined pan.

Using a tablespoon, spread fudge evenly throughout the pan and sprinkle the pecan pieces on top. Swirl final design into the fudge.

When fudge is firm, lift the foil and fudge from the pan and cut the fudge into desired size pieces. Place pieces on plate or platter that has been sprinkled lightly with coarse corn flake pieces or chopped nut meats, thus allowing the bottoms to "crust" up along with the sides.

Note: Your cooking time may vary. See page 23. ❖

Almost everyone likes cherries and strawberries.

In this fudge the two flavors have been combined to give you a colorful and delicious candy.

For a lot of us, our first experience with a maraschino cherry was when we bit into a cherry cordial or as it is more commonly called, a chocolate covered cherry. With this rendering the chocolate flavor has been replaced with strawberries. The smooth overtones of vanilla and butter have been retained.

This colorful, very sweet fudge will set your taste buds awhirl. ❖

CHERRY BERRY FUDGE

21/3   Cups granulated sugar
1   4.6 Oz. package JELL-O⁽ᴿ⁾ Brand Vanilla cook & serve pudding mix
2   Tablespoons all natural butter flavored sprinkles
4   Tablespoons instant non fat dry milk powder
3/4   Cup plus 2 tablespoons water
1/4   Cup maraschino cherries, drained & chopped
1   Teaspoon strawberry extract

If using an electric stove, preheat the largest burner to the highest heat prior to assembling ingredients in order to speed things up. Line a 6" by 8" by 2" pan or dish with aluminum foil. No need to veggie spray the foil.

Combine all ingredients in a 10 inch cast iron dutch oven. Place on preheated burner and bring to a full rolling boil while stirring continuously. Set an accurate timer for 4 minutes. (See note below). Continue to stir throughout the cooking process with a stainless steel whisk.

After boiling for the 4 minutes remove from heat and continue stirring until mixture stops boiling.

Set a sheet pan, approximately 10" by 15", on top of a cold wet towel (cold tap water is fine). Pour mixture onto the sheet pan. Using a plastic pastry scraper, spatula, or other flat utensil, move mixture around so as to combine and blend those fudge crystals beginning to form, in spots, on the bottom of the pan with the rest of the mixture.

After two or three minutes move sheet pan to a fresh cold towel and continue to scrape the fudging crystals from the bottom of the pan and to fold them into the mixture.

After a few minutes move pan to another cold towel and as mixture starts to thicken begin moving and accumulating the mixture to the corner of the pan from which you are going to pour mixture out into an aluminum foil lined pan approximately 6" by 8" by 2".

As mixture becomes very thick, pour out into the foil lined pan.

Using a tablespoon, spread fudge evenly throughout the pan. Swirl final design into the fudge.

When fudge is firm, lift the foil and fudge from the pan and cut the fudge into desired size pieces. Place pieces on plate or platter that has been sprinkled lightly with coarse corn flake pieces or chopped nut meats, thus allowing the bottoms to "crust" up along with the sides.

Note: Your cooking time may vary. See page 23. ❖

Your imaginative, creative juices flow best
in the morning after a brisk walk.

Late night creations are often peculiar
things to behold the next day.

BON BONS

❀

❀

This French Cream is the foundation of all of our Bon Bon fillings.

Just as Martha Washington and Dolly Madison relied on a french cream to heighten their guests gastronomic experience, our Bon Bons rely on the extra creamy and smooth character of this exciting, new and outrageous delight.

Your guests will surmise that you have fabricated this cream from powdered sugar. As the recipe demonstrates, you have not! They will "taste" real butter and cream, and in this they will be correct, however the fat has been removed.

After chilling in the freezer use a teaspoon and your hands to shape this filling into marble-size pieces for bon bon centers. Use some powdered sugar as a dusting to keep it from sticking to your hands.

The Guar gum can be purchased from most health food stores or you may order some from:

> The Food Bin
> 12268 Shawnee Mission Parkway
> Shawnee, Kansas 66216
>
> Telephone: 1-913-268 4103

FRENCH CREAM
(Bon Bon filling)

1 1/4	Cup granulated sugar
1	Tablespoon all natural butter flavored sprinkles
1	Teaspoon guar gum (See previous page)
1/2	Cup evaporated skimmed milk
1	Teaspoon clear imitation vanilla extract

If using an electric stove, preheat the largest burner to the highest heat prior to assembling ingredients in order to speed things up. Line a plate or platter with aluminum foil. No need to veggie spray the foil.

Combine all ingredients in a 10 inch cast iron skillet. Place on preheated burner and bring to a full rolling boil while stirring continuously. Set an accurate timer for 2 1/2 minutes. (See note below). Continue to stir throughout the cooking process with a stainless steel whisk.

After boiling for the 2 1/2 minutes remove from heat and continue stirring until mixture stops boiling.

Set a sheet pan, approximately 10" by 15", on top of a cold wet towel (cold tap water is fine). Pour mixture onto the sheet pan. Using a plastic pastry scraper, spatula, or other flat utensil, move mixture around so as to combine and blend those fudge crystals beginning to form, in spots, on the bottom of the pan with the rest of the mixture.

After two or three minutes move sheet pan to a fresh cold towel and continue to scrape the fudging crystals from the bottom of the pan and to fold them into the mixture.

After a few minutes move pan to another cold towel and as mixture starts to thicken begin moving and accumulating the mixture to the corner of the pan from which you are going to pour mixture out into the foil lined plate or platter.

As mixture becomes thick, pour out into the foil lined plate or platter.

Using a tablespoon, spread cream evenly.

When cream is firm, cut into desired size pieces.

Note: Your cooking time may vary. See page 23. ❖

With just one batch of Double Dutch Chocolate fudge from page 87 and one batch of French Cream Bon Bon filling from the previous recipe you can put together a beautiful assortment of delicious and colorful Bon Bons.

These tempting morsels are as real as the sunrise and as mouth-watering as you can imagine. They bring forth a peculiar response from folks who consider themselves on a fat-free diet. It requires a real stretch of the imagination to realize that this creamy, flavor-bursting bon bon center is fat free!

Don't worry, just enjoy and be sure that the French Cream centers are very cold and firm before dipping them into a hot melted coating fudge.

❀ When forming this cold candy into marble-size balls prior to dipping them, use a dusting of powdered sugar to keep them from sticking to your hands. Refrigerate again if necessary.

❀ For delicious mint patties just use mint extract for the flavoring and for peppermint Bon Bons use a peppermint extract.

❖

THE VARIETY CREAM
(Four Flavors of Cream From One Recipe)

Prepare one batch of French Cream from previous recipe and upon completion, divide into four portions. Place in four small individual pudding dishes or cups. Select your own desired flavors and prepare the individual dishes in an approximate manner as suggested in the following recipes. Use a fork to mash the firm French Cream and to mix the ingredients thoroughly.

ORANGE CREAM

1/4 French Cream Recipe (See previous Recipe)
1/4 Teaspoon orange extract
1   Teaspoon candied orange rind, finely chopped
4   Drops yellow food color
1   Drop Red food color

Combine and mix thoroughly. Cover with plastic wrap and place in freezer for at least an hour before use.

COCONUT CREAM

1/4 French Cream recipe (See previous recipe)
1/4 Teaspoon coconut extract
1   Teaspoon shredded coconut, finely chopped

Combine and mix thoroughly. Cover with plastic wrap and place in freezer for at least an hour before use.

MAPLE CREAM

1/4 French Cream recipe (See previous recipe)
1/4 Teaspoon Maple Flavor

Combine and mix thoroughly. Cover with plastic wrap and place in freezer for at least an hour before use.

PEANUT BUTTER CREAM

1/4 French Cream recipe (See previous recipe)
1/2 Teaspoon Watkins[R] Brand peanut butter flavoring
1   Teaspoon dry roasted peanuts, finely chopped

Combine and mix thoroughly. Cover with plastic wrap and place in freezer for at least an hour before use. ❖

A small box of assorted Truffles to give as a gift

A few Truffles left over to eat..

TRUFFLE FUDGE RECIPES

❀

Above: A Chocolate Orange Truffle

This fudge is oh so delicate with a smack of lemon to wake up any sleeping taste buds. It was designed to snuggle inside a tasty coating of the Double Dutch Chocolate Fudge found on page 87. With such a chocolate coating it becomes a Bon Bon or Truffle, however the chocolate coating is not necessary. If your desires are aimed toward the unusual & different, then certainly this lemony - butter fudge may well fill the bill. As part of a holiday fudge display it will markedly add color, variety, and character to your traditional food fare.

This fudge is a very soft fudge similar to the soft interior of a truffle. For a firmer fudge just increase the cooking time from 4 minutes to 4 1/2 minutes.

LEMON BUTTER TRUFFLE FUDGE

2 1/3 Cups granulated sugar
1   4.6 Oz. package JELL-O® Brand Vanilla cook & serve pudding mix
3   Tablespoons all natural butter flavored sprinkles
6   Tablespoons instant non fat dry milk powder
3   Tablespoons candied lemon rind
1   Teaspoon lemon extract
1   Cup plus 2 tablespoons water
3   Drops yellow food color

If using an electric stove, preheat the largest burner to the highest heat prior to assembling ingredients in order to speed things up. Line a 6" by 8" by 2" pan or dish with aluminum foil. No need to veggie spray the foil.

Combine all ingredients in a 10 inch cast iron dutch oven. Place on preheated burner and bring to a full rolling boil while stirring continuously. Set an accurate timer for 4 minutes. (See note below). Continue to stir throughout the cooking process with a stainless steel whisk.

After boiling for the 4 minutes remove from heat and continue stirring until mixture stops boiling.

Set a sheet pan approximately 10" by 15" on top of a cold wet towel (cold tap water is fine). Pour mixture onto the sheet pan. Using a plastic pastry scraper, spatula, or other flat utensil, move mixture around so as to combine and blend those fudge crystals beginning to form, in spots, on the bottom of the pan with the rest of the mixture.

After two or three minutes move sheet pan to a fresh cold towel and continue to scrape the fudging crystals from the bottom of the pan and to fold them into the mixture.

After a few minutes move pan to another cold towel and as mixture starts to thicken begin moving and accumulating the mixture to the corner of the pan from which you are going to pour mixture out into an aluminum foil lined pan approximately 6" by 8" by 2".

As mixture becomes very thick, pour out into the foil lined pan.

Using a tablespoon, spread fudge evenly throughout the pan. Swirl final design into the fudge.

When fudge is firm, lift the foil and fudge from the pan and cut the fudge into desired size pieces. Place pieces on plate or platter that has been sprinkled lightly with coarse corn flake pieces or chopped nut meats, thus allowing the bottoms to "crust" up along with the sides.

Note: Your cooking time may vary. See page 23. ❖

The first recorded evidence of a pineapple comes to us via the second voyage of Columbus, where it was noted among the wonders of the island of Guadaloupe, the strange tropical beauty of the 'Pina'. This was a fruit that to the Spanish explorers resembled a 'Pine' cone.

Somehow the pineapple was transported to Hawaii, the exact date is unknown, and today most of our pineapples are grown and processed there.

This fudge will provide you with an exhilarating center for your Bon Bons or Truffles.

Pineapple provides the zest, while butter and vanilla provide the smooth overtones of this fudge. With only 4 minutes boiling time this is quite a creamy fudge. When tucked inside a coating of Double Dutch Chocolate fudge (see page 87), and after a days rest, you have an excellent chocolate-coated pineapple truffle .

For a firmer fudge that will stand on its own, just increase the boiling time to 4 1/2 minutes.

For a stand-alone pineapple truffle, just be sure that crusts are allowed to form on all sides of your fudge, including the bottom. This can be accomplished by turning the pieces of fudge periodically and thereby allowing air to circulate around all sides and the bottom. ❖

PINEAPPLE CREAM TRUFFLE FUDGE

2 1/3 Cups granulated sugar
1   4.6 Oz. package JELL-O(R) Brand Vanilla cook & serve pudding mix
3   Tablespoons all natural butter flavored sprinkles
4   Tablespoons instant non fat dry milk powder
3   Tablespoons candied diced pineapple
1   Teaspoon pineapple extract
1   Cup plus 2 tablespoons water

If using an electric stove, preheat the largest burner to the highest heat prior to assembling ingredients in order to speed things up. Line a 6" by 8" by 2" pan or dish with aluminum foil. No need to veggie spray the foil.

Combine all ingredients in a 10 inch cast iron dutch oven. Place on preheated burner and bring to a full rolling boil while stirring continuously. Set an accurate timer for 4 1/2 minutes. (See note below). Continue to stir throughout the cooking process with a stainless steel whisk.

After boiling for the 4 1/2 minutes remove from heat and continue stirring until mixture stops boiling.

Set a sheet pan, approximately 10" by 15", on top of a cold wet towel (cold tap water is fine). Pour mixture onto the sheet pan. Using a plastic pastry scraper, spatula, or other flat utensil, move mixture around so as to combine and blend those fudge crystals beginning to form, in spots, on the bottom of the pan with the rest of the mixture.

After two or three minutes move sheet pan to a fresh cold towel and continue to scrape the fudging crystals from the bottom of the pan and to fold them into the mixture.

After a few minutes move pan to another cold towel and as mixture starts to thicken begin moving and accumulating the mixture to the corner of the pan from which you are going to pour mixture out into an aluminum foil lined pan approximately 6" by 8" by 2".

As mixture becomes very thick, pour out into the foil lined pan.

Using a tablespoon, spread fudge evenly throughout the pan. Swirl final design into the fudge.

When fudge is firm, lift the foil and fudge from the pan and cut the fudge into desired size pieces. Place pieces on plate or platter that has been sprinkled lightly with coarse corn flake pieces or chopped nut meats, thus allowing the bottoms to "crust" up along with the sides.

Note: Your cooking time may vary. See page 23. ❖

A master blend of good things!

Remember that box of chocolates of bygone days? Remember that one choice chocolate with the soft chocolate-orange filling? It was always a treat. This non fat fudge mimics that creamy center you found in chocolates past.

The arrogance of orange, the frisky nature of chocolate, the smoothness of butter and the mellowness of vanilla combine to create lasting memories of a truly memorable fudge.

For Truffles, simply coat these pieces of fudge with Double Dutch Chocolate Fudge (see page 87) and allow to sit around and rest for a day or more. Remember to turn the fudge occasionally so as to allow crusts to form on all sides.

For fudge that stands on its own, retaining the texture of fudge, just boil for an extra 1/2 minute. ❖

CHOCOLATE ORANGE TRUFFLE FUDGE

2 1/3 Cups granulated sugar
1   4.6 Oz. package JELL-O(R)Brand Vanilla cook & serve pudding mix
3   Tablespoons all natural butter flavored sprinkles
2   Tablespoons Dutch Processed European style cocoa
4   Tablespoons instant non fat dry milk powder
1/4   Cup Triple Sec Liqueur
1   Teaspoon orange extract
3   Tablespoons candied orange rind, finely chopped
3/4   Cup plus 2 tablespoons water

If using an electric stove, preheat the largest burner to the highest heat prior to assembling ingredients in order to speed things up. Line a 6" by 8" by 2" pan or dish with aluminum foil. No need to veggie spray the foil.

Combine all ingredients in a 10 inch cast iron dutch oven. Place on preheated burner and bring to a full rolling boil while stirring continuously. Set an accurate timer for 4 1/2 minutes. (See note below). Continue to stir throughout the cooking process with a stainless steel whisk.

After boiling for the 4 1/2 minutes remove from heat and continue stirring until mixture stops boiling.

Set a sheet pan, approximately 10" by 15", on top of a cold wet towel (cold tap water is fine). Pour mixture onto the sheet pan. Using a plastic pastry scraper, spatula, or other flat utensil, move mixture around so as to combine and blend those fudge crystals beginning to form, in spots, on the bottom of the pan with the rest of the mixture.

After two or three minutes move sheet pan to a fresh cold towel and continue to scrape the fudging crystals from the bottom of the pan and to fold them into the mixture.

After a few minutes move pan to another cold towel and as mixture starts to thicken begin moving and accumulating the mixture to the corner of the pan from which you are going to pour mixture out into an aluminum foil lined pan approximately 6" by 8" by 2".

As mixture becomes very thick, pour out into the foil lined pan.

Using a tablespoon, spread fudge evenly throughout the pan. Swirl final design into the fudge.

When fudge is firm, lift the foil and fudge from the pan and cut the fudge into desired size pieces. Place pieces on plate or platter that has been sprinkled lightly with coarse corn flake pieces or chopped nut meats, thus allowing the bottoms to "crust" up along with the sides.

Note: Your cooking time may vary. See page 23.❖

This is a liquered-up fudge truffle of the first magnitude.

The brashnesss of almonds rules the day with chocolate following a close second. For background you will find butter and vanilla adding to the spectrum of loving flavors.

Liquid Amaretto liqueur and strong almond extract transforms this chocolate from the ordinary into a luxurious, soft and smooth truffle. That almonds and chocolate go together has been a long known fact. This recipe renders them soul-mates without the interference of strangling fat.

This is another fudge designed to be the center of a chocolate Truffle and this job it accomplishes in a delightful fashion. After a days aging this fudge transforms itself into an unbelieveably creamy, soft texture, exactly as you would find inside an elegant, expensive truffle from your favorite chocolatier.

For use as a regular fudge just increase the boiling duration time by 1/2 minute and top with a tablespoon of chopped, sliced almonds. ❖

CHOCOLATE AMARETTO TRUFFLE FUDGE

2 1/3 Cups granulated sugar
1   4.6 Oz. package JELL-O(R) Brand Vanilla cook & serve pudding mix
3   Tablespoons all natural butter flavored sprinkles
2   Tablespoons Dutch Processed European style cocoa
4   Tablespoons instant non fat dry milk powder
3/4   Cup plus 2 tablespoons water
1/4   Cup Amaretto Liqueur
1   Teaspoon almond extract

If using an electric stove, preheat the largest burner to the highest heat prior to assembling ingredients in order to speed things up. Line a 6" by 8" by 2" pan or dish with aluminum foil. No need to veggie spray the foil.

Combine all ingredients in a 10 inch cast iron dutch oven. Place on preheated burner and bring to a full rolling boil while stirring continuously. Set an accurate timer for 3 minutes. (See note below). Continue to stir throughout the cooking process with a stainless steel whisk.

After boiling for the 3 minutes remove from heat and continue stirring until mixture stops boiling.

Set a sheet pan, approximately 10" by 15", on top of a cold wet towel (cold tap water is fine). Pour mixture onto the sheet pan. Using a plastic pastry scraper, spatula, or other flat utensil, move mixture around so as to combine and blend those fudge crystals beginning to form, in spots, on the bottom of the pan with the rest of the mixture.

After two or three minutes move sheet pan to a fresh cold towel and continue to scrape the fudging crystals from the bottom of the pan and to fold them into the mixture.

After a few minutes move pan to another cold towel and as mixture starts to thicken begin moving and accumulating the mixture to the corner of the pan from which you are going to pour mixture out into an aluminum foil lined pan approximately 6" by 8" by 2".

As mixture becomes very thick, pour out into the foil lined pan.

Using a tablespoon, spread fudge evenly throughout the pan. Swirl final design into the fudge.

When fudge is firm, lift the foil and fudge from the pan and cut the fudge into desired size pieces. Place pieces on plate or platter that has been sprinkled lightly with coarse corn flake pieces or chopped nut meats, thus allowing the bottoms to "crust" up along with the sides.

Note: Your cooking time may vary. See page 23.❖

The fact that these two flavors go together is indisputable. Coconut filled chocolate bars and Bon Bons have been popular for a long, long time. Here you'll find them coupled in a soft fudge, that, after a days rest will revert to a silky-smooth truffle.

Feel free to dip cubes of this fudge in the Double Dutch Chocolate Fudge found on page 87.

For a free standing Truffle, just be sure to allow pieces of this fudge to "crust" up on all sides and the bottom by periodically turning the pieces and allowing air to circulate around the fudge.

The shredded coconut in this recipe will add about 8 grams of fat to the entire batch of fudge and the coconut extract will add most of the flavor. If you don't care for the fatty coconut, then just double the amount of coconut extract and omit the shredded coconut. You will lose something in texture but nothing in flavor. ❖

CHOCOLATE COCONUT TRUFFLE FUDGE

2 1/3 Cups granulated sugar
1   4.6 Oz. package JELL-O(R) Brand Vanilla cook & serve pudding mix
3   Tablespoons all natural butter flavored sprinkles
2   Tablespoons Dutch Processed European style cocoa
4   Tablespoons instant non fat dry milk powder
1   Cup plus 2 tablespoons water
6   Tablespoons flake coconut
1   Teaspoon coconut extract

If using an electric stove, preheat the largest burner to the highest heat prior to assembling ingredients in order to speed things up. Line a 6" by 8" by 2" pan or dish with aluminum foil. No need to veggie spray the foil.

Except for the coconut extract, combine all ingredients in a 10 inch cast iron dutch oven. Place on preheated burner and bring to a full rolling boil while stirring continuously. Set an accurate timer for 4 1/2 minutes. (See note below). Continue to stir throughout the cooking process with a stainless steel whisk.

After boiling for the 4 1/2 minutes remove from heat and continue stirring until mixture stops boiling. **Add the coconut extract**.

Set a sheet pan, approximately 10" by 15", on top of a cold wet towel (cold tap water is fine). Pour mixture onto the sheet pan. Using a plastic pastry scraper, spatula, or other flat utensil, move mixture around so as to combine and blend those fudge crystals beginning to form, in spots, on the bottom of the pan with the rest of the mixture.

After two or three minutes move sheet pan to a fresh cold towel and continue to scrape the fudging crystals from the bottom of the pan and to fold them into the mixture.

After a few minutes move pan to another cold towel and as mixture starts to thicken begin moving and accumulating the mixture to the corner of the pan from which you are going to pour mixture out into an aluminum foil lined pan approximately 6" by 8" by 2".

As mixture becomes very thick, pour out into the foil lined pan.

Using a tablespoon, spread fudge evenly throughout the pan. Swirl final design into the fudge.

When fudge is firm, lift the foil and fudge from the pan and cut the fudge into desired size pieces. Place pieces on plate or platter that has been sprinkled lightly with coarse corn flake pieces or chopped nut meats, thus allowing the bottoms to "crust" up along with the sides.

Note: Your cooking time may vary. See page 23. ❖

I have very little flavor of my own,
I look like a nut,
I chop up like a nut,
and when properly prepared,
I fool everybody.

Who am I?

For the answer see page 25

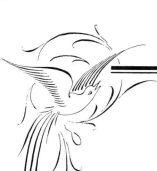

OLDE FASHIONED SUGARED FUDGE RECIPES

By combining the popular flavors of chocolate and peanut butter this recipe gives you a taste treat that many people, in this century, have fallen in love with.

The 1 tablespoon of Chunky 'Light' Peanut Butter adds about 6 grams of fat and provides some 'Nutty' texture. The 'Real' peanut butter flavor is provided by the Watkins(R) Brand Imitation Peanut Butter Flavor.

The 1/2 tablespoon of dry roasted peanuts adds about 2 or 3 grams of fat. The purpose of these peanuts is to decorate the top of the fudge and to alert the brain that this is a 'Peanutty' - Chocolate fudge.

The total fat content of this recipe is about 10 grams and the fat content, per 1 ounce serving, is less than one-half gram. ❖

CHOCOLATE PEANUT BUTTER FUDGE

2 1/3 Cups granulated sugar
1   4.6 Oz. package JELL-O(R) Brand Vanilla cook & serve pudding mix
3   Tablespoons all natural butter flavored sprinkles
2   Tablespoons Dutch Processed European style cocoa
4   Tablespoons instant non fat dry milk powder
1   Tablespoon Light Chunky peanut butter
1   Cup plus 2 tablespoons water
1   Teaspoon Watkins(R) Brand Imitation Peanut Butter Flavor
1/2   Tablespoon dry roasted peanuts, chopped

If using an electric stove, preheat the largest burner to the highest heat prior to assembling ingredients in order to speed things up. Line a 6" by 8" by 2" pan or dish with aluminum foil. No need to veggie spray the foil.

Except for the peanuts and the peanut butter flavor, combine all ingredients in a 10 inch cast iron dutch oven. Place on preheated burner and bring to a full rolling boil while stirring continuously. Set an accurate timer for 4 1/2 minutes. (See note below). Continue to stir throughout the cooking process with a stainless steel whisk.

After boiling for the 4 1/2 minutes remove from heat and continue stirring until mixture stops boiling. **Add the peanut butter flavor and stir to mix**.

Set a sheet pan, approximately 10" by 15", on top of a cold wet towel (cold tap water is fine). Pour mixture onto the sheet pan. Using a plastic pastry scraper, spatula, or other flat utensil, move mixture around so as to combine and blend those fudge crystals beginning to form, in spots, on the bottom of the pan with the rest of the mixture.

After two or three minutes move sheet pan to a fresh cold towel and continue to scrape the fudging crystals from the bottom of the pan and to fold them into the mixture.

After a few minutes move pan to another cold towel and as mixture starts to thicken begin moving and accumulating the mixture to the corner of the pan from which you are going to pour mixture out into an aluminum foil lined pan approximately 6" by 8" by 2".

As mixture becomes very thick, pour out into the foil lined pan.

Using a tablespoon, spread fudge evenly throughout the pan and **sprinkle the chopped peanuts** on top. Swirl final design into the fudge.

When fudge is firm, lift the foil and fudge from the pan and cut the fudge into desired size pieces. Place pieces on plate or platter that has been sprinkled lightly with coarse corn flake pieces or chopped nut meats, thus allowing the bottoms to "crust" up along with the sides.

Note: Your cooking time may vary. See page 23. ❖

As a small child, I remember my mother's pronouncement that Saturday would be the day for making fudge. This happy event occurred about every six months and was always preceded by a horse and wagon trip to town. The expectation of such a trip to town always meant an added measure of excitement.

It was the time of the great depression and what little money there was, was never spent foolishly. However, the purchasing of cocoa and extra sugar was deemed necessary in order to preserve the family's sanity. Maintaining one's sanity in the 1930's, while enduring rural Illinois tenant farm life, was not an easy task. The semi annual chocolate fudge brought a lot of fun and pure, simple enjoyment into a rather bleak and dismal life style.

It really didn't matter that the fudge almost never turned out to be real fudge. It was almost always a runny taffy-like mixture that was eaten with a spoon. But when it did turn out right, it was wonderful fudge that could be cut into pieces, picked up with the fingers and eaten as proper fudge.

The fudge from this recipe perfectly mimics the good batches of fudge we experienced during those depression days.

In this recipe the pecans add about 4 grams of fat, bringing the total recipe fat count to about 10 grams or less than 1/2 gram per serving. ❖

CHOCOLATE PECAN FUDGE

2 1/3 Cups granulated sugar
1   4.6 Oz. package JELL-O® Brand Vanilla cook & serve pudding mix
4   Tablespoons all natural butter flavored sprinkles
4   Tablespoons Dutch Processed European style cocoa
4   Tablespoons instant non fat dry milk powder
3/4   Cup plus 2 tablespoons water
1   Cup "Nut Meats", see page 25
1   Teaspoon pecan flavor
1/2   Tablespoon small pecan pieces

If using an electric stove, preheat the largest burner to the highest heat prior to assembling ingredients in order to speed things up. Line a 6" by 8" by 2" pan or dish with aluminum foil. No need to veggie spray the foil.

Except for the pecan flavor and the pecan pieces, combine all ingredients in a 10 inch cast iron dutch oven. Place on preheated burner and bring to a full rolling boil while stirring continuously. Set an accurate timer for 4 1/2 minutes. (See note below). Continue to stir throughout the cooking process with a stainless steel whisk.

After boiling for the 4 1/2 minutes remove from heat and continue stirring until mixture stops boiling. **Add the pecan flavor and stir**.

Set a sheet pan, approximately 10" by 15", on top of a cold wet towel (cold tap water is fine). Pour mixture onto the sheet pan. Using a plastic pastry scraper, spatula, or other flat utensil, move mixture around so as to combine and blend those fudge crystals beginning to form, in spots, on the bottom of the pan with the rest of the mixture.

After two or three minutes move sheet pan to a fresh cold towel and continue to scrape the fudging crystals from the bottom of the pan and to fold them into the mixture.

After a few minutes move pan to another cold towel and as mixture starts to thicken begin moving and accumulating the mixture to the corner of the pan from which you are going to pour mixture out into an aluminum foil lined pan approximately 6" by 8" by 2".

As mixture becomes very thick, pour out into the foil lined pan.

Using a tablespoon, spread fudge evenly throughout the pan and **sprinkle the pecan pieces on top**. Swirl final design into the fudge.

When fudge is firm, lift the foil and fudge from the pan and cut the fudge into desired size pieces. Place pieces on plate or platter that has been sprinkled lightly with coarse corn flake pieces or chopped nut meats, thus allowing the bottoms to "crust" up along with the sides.

Note: Your cooking time may vary. See page 23. ❖

Of all candy flavors chocolate is without a doubt the most popular.

"Dutch" chocolate refers to a processing technique whereby alkalis are added in order to neutralize the naturally occurring strong acids that are found in cocoa. This process makes the cocoa much smoother.

With this fudge you add an extra portion of dutch cocoa in order to intensify the chocolate flavor. When combined with milk, sugar and vanilla the aroma, of this fudge cooking, becomes soothing and satisfying to the soul.

Since this recipe contains only about 4 grams of fat, feel free to top dress it with a scant tablespoon of your favorite chopped nut, or use it as a Bon Bon or Truffle coating (see page 51).

Fruity Note:
For an outrageous Deep Velvet Chocolate Raspberry Fudge, replace 1 cup of water with 1 cup of pureed fresh frozen raspberries with juice (seeds removed if desired). Reduce the boiling time to 4 minutes. Be sure to add the 2 tablespoons of water that is called for. This fudge is best the second day after the flavors have merged. ❖

Milk Chocolate Note:
For Milk Chocolate Fudge just reduce the cocoa from 4 tablespoons to 1 tablespoon.

DOUBLE DUTCH CHOCOLATE FUDGE

2 1/3 Cups granulated sugar
1   4.6 Oz. package JELL-O(R) Brand Vanilla cook & serve pudding mix
4   Tablespoons all natural butter flavored sprinkles
4   Tablespoons Dutch Processed European style cocoa
4   Tablespoons instant non fat dry milk powder
1   Cup plus 2 tablespoons water

If using an electric stove, preheat the largest burner to the highest heat prior to assembling ingredients in order to speed things up. Line a 6" by 8" by 2" pan or dish with aluminum foil. No need to veggie spray the foil.

Combine all ingredients in a 10 inch cast iron dutch oven. Place on preheated burner and bring to a full rolling boil while stirring continuously. Set an accurate timer for 4 1/2 minutes. (See note below). Continue to stir throughout the cooking process with a stainless steel whisk.

After boiling for the 4 1/2 minutes remove from heat and continue stirring until mixture stops boiling.

Set a sheet pan, approximately 10" by 15", on top of a cold wet towel (cold tap water is fine). Pour mixture onto the sheet pan. Using a plastic pastry scraper, spatula, or other flat utensil, move mixture around so as to combine and blend those fudge crystals beginning to form, in spots, on the bottom of the pan with the rest of the mixture.

After two or three minutes move sheet pan to a fresh cold towel and continue to scrape the fudging crystals from the bottom of the pan and to fold them into the mixture.

After a few minutes move pan to another cold towel and as mixture starts to thicken begin moving and accumulating the mixture to the corner of the pan from which you are going to pour mixture out into an aluminum foil lined pan approximately 6" by 8" by 2".

As mixture becomes very thick, pour out into the foil lined pan.

Using a tablespoon, spread fudge evenly throughout the pan. Swirl final design into the fudge.

When fudge is firm, lift the foil and fudge from the pan and cut the fudge into desired size pieces. Place pieces on plate or platter that has been sprinkled lightly with coarse corn flake pieces or chopped nut meats, thus allowing the bottoms to "crust" up along with the sides.

Note: Your cooking time may vary. See page 23.❖

As you gaze down upon this finished jewel your mind will naturally question the reality of this being a truly no fat fudge. It is!

Is that not shredded coconut protrubing in abundance?

Are those not chunks of real pecans, clearly visible?

The answer to both questions is, yes.

Your mind, upon seeing the strikingly beautiful image this fudge projects, immediately starts to conjure up rememberances of the fine flavors of a sterling german chocolate cake from bygone days. Those flavors and textures are found in exuberant plenitude in this fudge.

The coconut adds about 6 grams of fat and the pecans add about another 4 grams of fat, but by placing them on top of the fudge in clear view for your eyes to see and your mind to relish, you have created an illusion of opulence which becomes reality with your first bite. The flavors and textures your mind expects are in this fudge. It is a full bodied, exuberant fudge fullfilling all of your expectations.

Remember, by government regulation, when you reduce the per serving fat content to less than 1/2 gram you may call your product no-fat, non-fat or fat free. The total fat content of this recipe is about 11 grams and when you cut it into 24 individual pieces each piece or serving contains less than 1/2 gram of fat.

Nutty Note:

To prepare the 'Nut Meats' called for in the next recipe, soak dry garbonzos over night and then next day bring to a boil and boil for only 15 minutes. Remove from heat, drain, rinse, and towel-dry. Place in a food processor and chop into the size of pecan pieces. The husks assume the texture of coconut and the interior becomes "Nut Meats". ❖

GERMAN CHOCOLATE FUDGE

21/3 Cups granulated sugar
1   4.6 Oz. package JELL-O(R) Brand Vanilla cook & serve pudding mix
3   Tablespoons all natural butter flavored sprinkles
1   Tablespoon Dutch Processed European style cocoa
4   Tablespoons instant non fat dry milk powder
1/4 Cup flake coconut, loosely packed
1   Cup plus 2 tablespoons water
1   Teaspoon Pecan flavor
1   Teaspoon coconut flavor
1/4 Cup "Nut Meats" (See Nutty Note on previous page)
1/2 Tablespoon pecans, chopped

If using an electric stove, preheat the largest burner to the highest heat prior to assembling ingredients in order to speed things up. Line a 6" by 8" by 2" pan or dish with aluminum foil. No need to veggie spray the foil.

Set aside 1 tablespoon shreded coconut and the pecans. Combine all other ingredients in a 10 inch cast iron dutch oven. Place on preheated burner and bring to a full rolling boil while stirring continuously. Set an accurate timer for 4 1/2 minutes. (See note below). Continue to stir throughout the cooking process with a stainless steel whisk.

After boiling for the 4 1/2 minutes remove from heat and continue stirring until mixture stops boiling.

Set a sheet pan approximately 10" by 15" on top of a cold wet towel (cold tap water is fine). Pour mixture onto the sheet pan. Using a plastic pastry scraper, spatula, or other flat utensil, move mixture around so as to combine and blend those fudge crystals beginning to form, in spots, on the bottom of the pan with the rest of the mixture.

After two or three minutes move sheet pan to a fresh cold towel and continue to scrape the fudging crystals from the bottom of the pan and to fold them into the mixture.

After a few minutes move pan to another cold towel and as mixture starts to thicken begin moving and accumulating the mixture to the corner of the pan from which you are going to pour mixture out into an aluminum foil lined pan approximately 6" by 8" by 2".

As mixture becomes very thick, pour out into the foil lined pan. ❀ Using a tablespoon, spread fudge evenly throughout the pan. Sprinkle on the 1 tablespoon of coconut that you set aside and the 1/2 tablespoon of chopped pecans. Swirl final design into the fudge.

When fudge is firm, lift the foil and fudge from the pan and cut the fudge into desired size pieces. Place pieces on plate or platter that has been sprinkled lightly with coarse corn flake pieces or chopped nut meats, thus allowing the bottoms to "crust" up along with the sides.

Note: Your cooking time may vary. See page 23. ❖

The real peanut butter in this fudge adds a little to the flavor, some to the texture and gives the perception of authenticity.

The real flavor "bang" comes from the Watkins[R] Brand, Imitation Peanut Butter Flavor.

It is the combining of the old fashioned with the new that allows you to indulge in a more healthful peanut butter fudge.

Just be sure that the "Light" peanut butter you use contains no more than 6 grams of fat per tablespoon. ❖

Above: That is Real Peanut Butter Fudge sandwiched between layers of Double Dutch Chocolate Fudge.

REAL PEANUT BUTTER FUDGE
(Also contains artificial flavor)

2 1/3 Cups granulated sugar
1   4.6 Oz. package JELL-O⁽ᴿ⁾ Brand Vanilla cook & serve pudding mix
3   Tablespoons all natural butter flavored sprinkles
1   Tablespoon light peanut butter
4   Tablespoons instant non fat dry milk powder
1   Cup plus 2 tablespoons water
1   Teaspoon Watkins⁽ᴿ⁾ Brand Peanut Butter Flavor

If using an electric stove, preheat the largest burner to the highest heat prior to assembling ingredients in order to speed things up. Line a 6" by 8" by 2" pan or dish with aluminum foil. No need to veggie spray the foil.

Except for the peanut butter flavor, combine all ingredients in a 10 inch cast iron dutch oven. Place on preheated burner and bring to a full rolling boil while stirring continuously. Set an accurate timer for 4 1/2 minutes. (See note below). Continue to stir throughout the cooking process with a stainless steel whisk.

After boiling for the 4 1/2 minutes remove from heat and continue stirring until mixture stops boiling. **Add the peanut butter flavor.**

Set a sheet pan, approximately 10" by 15", on top of a cold wet towel (cold tap water is fine). Pour mixture onto the sheet pan. Using a plastic pastry scraper, spatula, or other flat utensil, move mixture around so as to combine and blend those fudge crystals beginning to form, in spots, on the bottom of the pan with the rest of the mixture.

After two or three minutes move sheet pan to a fresh cold towel and continue to scrape the fudging crystals from the bottom of the pan and to fold them into the mixture.

After a few minutes move pan to another cold towel and as mixture starts to thicken begin moving and accumulating the mixture to the corner of the pan from which you are going to pour mixture out into an aluminum foil lined pan approximately 6" by 8" by 2".

As mixture becomes very thick, pour out into the foil lined pan.

Using a tablespoon, spread fudge evenly throughout the pan. Swirl final design into the fudge.

When fudge is firm, lift the foil and fudge from the pan and cut the fudge into desired size pieces. Place pieces on plate or platter that has been sprinkled lightly with coarse corn flake pieces or chopped nut meats, thus allowing the bottoms to "crust" up along with the sides.

Note: Your cooking time may vary. See page 23. ❖

Have you heard? Miss Vanilla and Mr. Pecan are going steady and this fudge has to be one of the reasons why.

Certainly they are compatible. Although different individuals, when matched together they elevate the combined flavor to a higher level.

Vanilla is good.

Pecans are good.

Vanilla-Pecan fudge is great! ❖

Above: Pieces of Vanilla Pecan Fudge with a few raisins thrown in for good measure.

VANILLA PECAN FUDGE

2 1/3 Cups granulated sugar
1   4.6 Oz. package JELL-O(R) Brand Vanilla cook & serve pudding mix
3   Tablespoons all natural butter flavored sprinkles
2   Tablespoons instant non fat dry milk powder
1   Cup plus 2 tablespoons evaporated skimmed milk
1   Teaspoon pecan flavor
1   Tablespoon pecan pieces

If using an electric stove, preheat the largest burner to the highest heat prior to assembling ingredients in order to speed things up. Line a 6" by 8" by 2" pan or dish with aluminum foil. No need to veggie spray the foil.

Except for the pecan flavor and the pecan pieces, combine all ingredients in a 10 inch cast iron dutch oven. Place on preheated burner and bring to a full rolling boil while stirring continuously. Set an accurate timer for 3 1/2 minutes. (See note below). Continue to stir throughout the cooking process with a stainless steel whisk.

After boiling for the 3 1/2 minutes remove from heat and continue stirring until mixture stops boiling. **Add the pecan flavor and stir to mix**.

Set a sheet pan, approximately 10" by 15", on top of a cold wet towel (cold tap water is fine). Pour mixture onto the sheet pan. Using a plastic pastry scraper, spatula, or other flat utensil, move mixture around so as to combine and blend those fudge crystals beginning to form, in spots, on the bottom of the pan with the rest of the mixture.

After two or three minutes move sheet pan to a fresh cold towel and continue to scrape the fudging crystals from the bottom of the pan and to fold them into the mixture.

After a few minutes move pan to another cold towel and as mixture starts to thicken begin moving and accumulating the mixture to the corner of the pan from which you are going to pour mixture out into an aluminum foil lined pan approximately 6" by 8" by 2".

As mixture becomes very thick, pour out into the foil lined pan.

Using a tablespoon, spread fudge evenly throughout the pan and **sprinkle the pecan pieces on top.** Swirl final design into the fudge.

When fudge is firm, lift the foil and fudge from the pan and cut the fudge into desired size pieces. Place pieces on plate or platter that has been sprinkled lightly with coarse corn flake pieces or chopped nut meats, thus allowing the bottoms to "crust" up along with the sides.

Note: Your cooking time may vary. See page 23. ❖

Real brandy sets this fudge aglow and the pungency of the orange awakens all the taste buds.

With your first bite of this fine-grained, smooth fudge comes disbelief.

How can this gift from above be fat-free?

The answer:

> Mine is not to question why
> Mine is just to eat and enjoy. ❖

CHANTILLY CREAM FUDGE

2 1/3 Cups granulated sugar
1   4.6 Oz. package JELL-O(R) Brand Vanilla cook & serve pudding mix
2   Tablespoons all natural butter flavored sprinkles
1/4   Cup brandy
2   Tablespoons Triple Sec Liqueur
3/4   Cup plus 2 tablespoons evaporated skimmed milk
1   Teaspoon orange extract

If using an electric stove, preheat the largest burner to the highest heat prior to assembling ingredients in order to speed things up. Line a 6" by 8" by 2" pan or dish with aluminum foil. No need to veggie spray the foil.

Except for the orange extract, combine all ingredients in a 10 inch cast iron dutch oven. Place on preheated burner and bring to a full rolling boil while stirring continuously. Set an accurate timer for 4 minutes. (See note below). Continue to stir throughout the cooking process with a stainless steel whisk.

After boiling for the 4 minutes remove from heat and continue stirring until mixture stops boiling. **Add the orange extract.**

Set a sheet pan, approximately 10" by 15", on top of a cold wet towel (cold tap water is fine). Pour mixture onto the sheet pan. Using a plastic pastry scraper, spatula, or other flat utensil, move mixture around so as to combine and blend those fudge crystals beginning to form, in spots, on the bottom of the pan with the rest of the mixture.

After two or three minutes move sheet pan to a fresh cold towel and continue to scrape the fudging crystals from the bottom of the pan and to fold them into the mixture.

After a few minutes move pan to another cold towel and as mixture starts to thicken begin moving and accumulating the mixture to the corner of the pan from which you are going to pour mixture out into an aluminum foil lined pan approximately 6" by 8" by 2".

As mixture becomes very thick, pour out into the foil lined pan.

Using a tablespoon, spread fudge evenly throughout the pan. Swirl final design into the fudge.

When fudge is firm, lift the foil and fudge from the pan and cut the fudge into desired size pieces. Place pieces on plate or platter that has been sprinkled lightly with coarse corn flake pieces or chopped nut meats, thus allowing the bottoms to "crust" up along with the sides.

Note: Your cooking time may vary. See page 23. ❖

Wow! This fudge stokes your "Get up and Go" with a gentle portion of caffeine and a giant portion of exciting flavor.

If you like the flavor of coffee, you'll love it more, as combined here, with this creamy, buttery-rich, vanilla ensemble.

The only thing missing is the fat and I'm sure you won't miss it, as this is a smooth, creamy, melt-in-your-mouth, delicate fudge.

This fudge has been described as a fudge for discriminating tastes. ❖

Above: Cappuccino Fudge

CAPPUCCINO FUDGE

2 1/3 Cups granulated sugar
1   4.6 Oz. package JELL-O^(R) Brand Vanilla cook & serve pudding mix
3   Tablespoons all natural butter flavored sprinkles
2/3   Cup plus 2 tablespoons evaporated skimmed milk
1/3   Cup your favorite fresh brewed expresso coffee

If using an electric stove, preheat the largest burner to the highest heat prior to assembling ingredients in order to speed things up. Line a 6" by 8" by 2" pan or dish with aluminum foil. No need to veggie spray the foil.

Combine all ingredients in a 10 inch cast iron dutch oven. Place on preheated burner and bring to a full rolling boil while stirring continuously. Set an accurate timer for 4 1/2 minutes. (See note below). Continue to stir throughout the cooking process with a stainless steel whisk.

After boiling for the 4 1/2 minutes remove from heat and continue stirring until mixture stops boiling.

Set a sheet pan, approximately 10" by 15", on top of a cold wet towel (cold tap water is fine). Pour mixture onto the sheet pan. Using a plastic pastry scraper, spatula, or other flat utensil, move mixture around so as to combine and blend those fudge crystals beginning to form, in spots, on the bottom of the pan with the rest of the mixture.

After two or three minutes move sheet pan to a fresh cold towel and continue to scrape the fudging crystals from the bottom of the pan and to fold them into the mixture.

After a few minutes move pan to another cold towel and as mixture starts to thicken begin moving and accumulating the mixture to the corner of the pan from which you are going to pour mixture out into an aluminum foil lined pan approximately 6" by 8" by 2".

As mixture becomes very thick, pour out into the foil lined pan.

Using a tablespoon, spread fudge evenly throughout the pan. Swirl final design into the fudge.

When fudge is firm, lift the foil and fudge from the pan and cut the fudge into desired size pieces. Place pieces on plate or platter that has been sprinkled lightly with coarse corn flake pieces or chopped nut meats, thus allowing the bottoms to "crust" up along with the sides.

Note: Your cooking time may vary. See page 23. ❖

Rum was originally called "The Comfortable Waters" by the English. In the West Indies a crude form was called "Kill Devil". Needless to say the name "Kill Devil" was hard to market and so somewhere along the way this brew, made by fermenting molasses, became known as "Rum".

In this recipe you'll find rum flavors comfortably balanced with butter and vanilla.

PS: The darker the rum, the more intense the flavor. ❖

Above: That's Butter Rum Fudge with an Art Deco finish, accomplished by pouring a small amount of melted Double Dutch Chocolate Fudge on top before the fudge is set and then applying the final swirls.

BUTTER RUM FUDGE

2 1/3 Cups granulated sugar
1   4.6 Oz. package JELL-O⁽ᴿ⁾ Brand Vanilla cook & serve pudding mix
4   Tablespoons all natural butter flavored sprinkles
4   Tablespoons instant non fat dry milk powder
3/4   Cup plus 2 tablespoons water
1/4   Cup dark rum
1   Teaspoon rum flavor

If using an electric stove, preheat the largest burner to the highest heat prior to assembling ingredients in order to speed things up. Line a 6" by 8" by 2" pan or dish with aluminum foil. No need to veggie spray the foil.

Except for the rum flavor, combine all ingredients in a 10 inch cast iron dutch oven. Place on preheated burner and bring to a full rolling boil while stirring continuously. Set an accurate timer for 4 1/2 minutes. (See note below). Continue to stir throughout the cooking process with a stainless steel whisk.

After boiling for the 4 1/2 minutes remove from heat and continue stirring until mixture stops boiling. **Add the rum flavor and stir.**

Set a sheet pan, approximately 10" by 15", on top of a cold wet towel (cold tap water is fine). Pour mixture onto the sheet pan. Using a plastic pastry scraper, spatula, or other flat utensil, move mixture around so as to combine and blend those fudge crystals beginning to form, in spots, on the bottom of the pan with the rest of the mixture.

After two or three minutes move sheet pan to a fresh cold towel and continue to scrape the fudging crystals from the bottom of the pan and to fold them into the mixture.

After a few minutes move pan to another cold towel and as mixture starts to thicken begin moving and accumulating the mixture to the corner of the pan from which you are going to pour mixture out into an aluminum foil lined pan approximately 6" by 8" by 2".

As mixture becomes very thick, pour out into the foil lined pan.

Using a tablespoon, spread fudge evenly throughout the pan. Swirl final design into the fudge.

When fudge is firm, lift the foil and fudge from the pan and cut the fudge into desired size pieces. Place pieces on plate or platter that has been sprinkled lightly with coarse corn flake pieces or chopped nut meats, thus allowing the bottoms to "crust" up along with the sides.

Note: Your cooking time may vary. See page 23. ❖

I always believed that the original Mocha came about as a result of someone drinking their cocoa from a dirty coffee cup. With the pleasant mingling of those two flavors that person was onto something that still pervades our menus and cookbooks.

You might want to experiment with this recipe by substituting fresh brewed coffee for the water and omitting the instant coffee. By doing this you are sure to have the coffee flavor that you most appreciate. The flavored, exotic coffees should gladly impart their uniqueness to this fudge.

This is a delightful "Tea Time" fudge that is sure to bring forth the 'oohs' and 'ahs'. ❖

MOCHA FUDGE

2 1/3 Cups granulated sugar
1   4.6 Oz. package JELL-O(R) Brand Vanilla cook & serve pudding mix
2   Tablespoons all natural butter flavored sprinkles
1   Tablespoon Dutch Processed European style cocoa
4   Tablespoons instant non fat dry milk powder
1   Cup plus 2 tablespoons water
1   Tablespoon instant coffee powder

If using an electric stove, preheat the largest burner to the highest heat prior to assembling ingredients in order to speed things up. Line a 6" by 8" by 2" pan or dish with aluminum foil. No need to veggie spray the foil.

Combine all ingredients in a 10 inch cast iron dutch oven. Place on preheated burner and bring to a full rolling boil while stirring continuously. Set an accurate timer for 4 1/2 minutes. (See note below). Continue to stir throughout the cooking process with a stainless steel whisk.

After boiling for the 4 1/2 minutes remove from heat and continue stirring until mixture stops boiling.

Set a sheet pan, approximately 10" by 15", on top of a cold wet towel (cold tap water is fine). Pour mixture onto the sheet pan. Using a plastic pastry scraper, spatula, or other flat utensil, move mixture around so as to combine and blend those fudge crystals beginning to form, in spots, on the bottom of the pan with the rest of the mixture.

After two or three minutes move sheet pan to a fresh cold towel and continue to scrape the fudging crystals from the bottom of the pan and to fold them into the mixture.

After a few minutes move pan to another cold towel and as mixture starts to thicken begin moving and accumulating the mixture to the corner of the pan from which you are going to pour mixture out into an aluminum foil lined pan approximately 6" by 8" by 2".

As mixture becomes very thick, pour out into the foil lined pan.

Using a tablespoon, spread fudge evenly throughout the pan. Swirl final design into the fudge.

When fudge is firm, lift the foil and fudge from the pan and cut the fudge into desired size pieces. Place pieces on plate or platter that has been sprinkled lightly with coarse corn flake pieces or chopped nut meats, thus allowing the bottoms to "crust" up along with the sides.

Note: Your cooking time may vary. See page 23. ❖

The shredded coconut in this recipe adds about 8 grams of fat and a lot of texture. The coconut extract adds tons of flavor. Between the two of them, you will find, a truly substantial candy that will satisfy your craving for coconut and fudge.

By the way, it is all right to use imitation extract.

For an interesting Bon Bon, try coating pieces of this fudge with melted Double Dutch Chocolate fudge from page 87. ❖

COCONUT CREAM FUDGE

2 1/3 Cups granulated sugar
1   4.6 Oz. package JELL-O⁽ᴿ⁾ Brand Vanilla cook & serve pudding mix
4   Tablespoons all natural butter flavored sprinkles
4   Tablespoons instant non fat dry milk powder
1   Cup plus 2 tablespoons water
1/3   Cup flake coconut
1   Teaspoon coconut extract

If using an electric stove, preheat the largest burner to the highest heat prior to assembling ingredients in order to speed things up. Line a 6" by 8" by 2" pan or dish with aluminum foil. No need to veggie spray the foil.

Except for the coconut extract, combine all ingredients in a 10 inch cast iron dutch oven. Place on preheated burner and bring to a full rolling boil while stirring continuously. Set an accurate timer for 4 1/2 minutes. (See note below). Continue to stir throughout the cooking process with a stainless steel whisk.

After boiling for the 4 1/2 minutes remove from heat and continue stirring until mixture stops boiling. Add the coconut extract and stir.

Set a sheet pan, approximately 10" by 15", on top of a cold wet towel (cold tap water is fine). Pour mixture onto the sheet pan. Using a plastic pastry scraper, spatula, or other flat utensil, move mixture around so as to combine and blend those fudge crystals beginning to form, in spots, on the bottom of the pan with the rest of the mixture.

After two or three minutes move sheet pan to a fresh cold towel and continue to scrape the fudging crystals from the bottom of the pan and to fold them into the mixture.

After a few minutes move pan to another cold towel and as mixture starts to thicken begin moving and accumulating the mixture to the corner of the pan from which you are going to pour mixture out into an aluminum foil lined pan approximately 6" by 8" by 2".

As mixture becomes very thick, pour out into the foil lined pan.

Using a tablespoon, spread fudge evenly throughout the pan. Swirl final design into the fudge.

When fudge is firm, lift the foil and fudge from the pan and cut the fudge into desired size pieces. Place pieces on plate or platter that has been sprinkled lightly with coarse corn flake pieces or chopped nut meats, thus allowing the bottoms to "crust" up along with the sides.

Note: Your cooking time may vary. See page 23. ❖

Poof! The magic wand of Watkins(R) Brand products and their remarkable Imitation Peanut Butter Flavor returns you to yesteryear when you didn't know that real peanut butter was half fat and you enjoyed it in ignorance. (Albeit in a fatter state)

Now you can enjoy this flavorful, buttery, decadent, Chunky Peanut Butter Fudge without the fat or the accompanying guilt. It doesn't stick to the roof of your mouth either. ❖

Above: Peanut Butter Fudge is great by itself or in the company of Double Dutch Chocolate.

104

CHUNKY NO PEANUT BUTTER FUDGE

2 1/3 Cups granulated sugar
1   4.6 Oz. package JELL-O⁽ᴿ⁾ Brand Vanilla cook & serve pudding mix
2   Tablespoons all natural butter flavored sprinkles
1   Cup "Nut Meats" from page 25
3/4   Cup evaporated skimmed milk
2   Teaspoons Watkins⁽ᴿ⁾ Brand imitation peanut butter flavor
1   Tablespoon oven roasted peanuts, chopped

If using an electric stove, preheat the largest burner to the highest heat prior to assembling ingredients in order to speed things up. Line a 6" by 8" by 2" pan or dish with aluminum foil. No need to veggie spray the foil.

Except for the peanuts and 1 teaspoon peanut butter flavor, combine all ingredients in a 10 inch cast iron dutch oven. Place on preheated burner and bring to a full rolling boil while stirring continuously. Set an accurate timer for 4 1/2 minutes. (See note below). Continue to stir throughout the cooking process with a stainless steel whisk.

After boiling for the 4 1/2 minutes remove from heat and continue stirring until mixture stops boiling. **Add 1 teaspoon peanut butter flavor and stir to mix**.

Set a sheet pan, approximately 10" by 15", on top of a cold wet towel (cold tap water is fine). Pour mixture onto the sheet pan. Using a plastic pastry scraper, spatula, or other flat utensil, move mixture around so as to combine and blend those fudge crystals beginning to form, in spots, on the bottom of the pan with the rest of the mixture.

After two or three minutes move sheet pan to a fresh cold towel and continue to scrape the fudging crystals from the bottom of the pan and to fold them into the mixture.

After a few minutes move pan to another cold towel and as mixture starts to thicken begin moving and accumulating the mixture to the corner of the pan from which you are going to pour mixture out into an aluminum foil lined pan approximately 6" by 8" by 2".

As mixture becomes very thick, pour out into the foil lined pan.

Using a tablespoon, spread fudge evenly throughout the pan and **sprinkle the peanuts on top**. Swirl final design into the fudge.

When fudge is firm, lift the foil and fudge from the pan and cut the fudge into desired size pieces. Place pieces on plate or platter that has been sprinkled lightly with coarse corn flake pieces or chopped nut meats, thus allowing the bottoms to "crust" up along with the sides.

Note: Your cooking time may vary. See page 23. ❖

105

Above: The beginning of a filigree finish on a plate of marshmallow Chocolate Mint Fudge. This finish is accomplished by placing the bottom of a spoon in the sticky, unset fudge, drawing the spoon up in the air and setting it down on the other side and repeating until the fudge is firm.

Below: The same batch of fudge with a different finish. The center is solid and the outer edges that firm up last are being tucked in and up.

MARSHMALLOW FUDGE RECIPES

The Post® Great Grains®, Whole Grain Cereal with Double Pecans, used in this recipe, brings a powerful lot of crunch and flavor to this fudge.

We all know of the wonderful attributes of chocolate, so use your imagination to visualize combining it with vanilla, butter, marshmallows, pecans and Great Grains®.

This fudge is best eaten the first couple of days. ❖

CHOCOLATE PECAN CRUNCH FUDGE

1   3.4 Ounce package JELL-O(R) Brand chocolate cook and serve pudding mix
11/2 Cups granulated sugar
2   Tablespoon all natural butter-flavored sprinkles
1/2   Cup plus 2 Tablespoons evaporated skimmed milk
1   Teaspoon pecan extract
5   Cups miniature marshmallows
1   Cup Post(R) Great Grains(R) Cereal, Double Pecan

Except for the marshmallows and cereal, place ingredients in a 10" cast iron skillet. Place your stainless steel whisk next to the stove. Before we begin cooking the candy, let's prepare some other items.

Prepare a plate or platter by spraying it with butter flavored vegetable spray and set it on a wire cooling rack. Next, measure the marshmallows and set them in front of the hand mixer. You'll need several tablespoons so get them out and have them handy.

Ok, let's start cooking. Place skillet on a large electric burner which is set to the hottest temperature. If using a gas stove, turn it to full on. Mix and stir continously.

When mixture comes to a full rolling boil, set an accurate timer to 5 minutes and continue stirring.

After 5 minutes, remove the skillet from the hot burner and continue stirring until mixture no longer boils.

Add marshmallows and combine using a tablespoon to mix marshmallows and the hot mixture. You can't use the hand mixer at first because the melting marshmallows will climb up the beaters and refuse to come down. By using a tablespoon first the mixture is somewhat thinned and now you can use the hand mixer effectively. Mix until smooth and the marshmallows are melted. (About a minute or so)

Add cereal, mix well with a tablespoon, and pour mixture out onto the veggie sprayed plate or platter and place it on a wire rack to cool.

Check your candy every few minutes by swirling the top. Shortly, (usually within 10 to 30 minutes) these swirls will begin to hold their shape. Apply your final pattern or design.

Use a butter knife to raise and shape the edges of your fudge. Remember, the outer edges will set up last.

When set, use a thin bladed knife to score or cut the fudge. Cover with plastic wrap and store what's left after you have appropriately sampled your fudge. ❖

An olde, olde town in Vermont with its cobblestone streets and its folksy Bed and Breakfast Inn is a cherished memory for many people.

The look of this fudge after the whole, miniature marshmallows on the bottom have risen up through the warm mixture to the top, will evoke rememberances of those cobble stone streets and the taste will remind you of the sweetness of those memories.

If you don't have these memories find someone who has and is willing to share them with you. Better yet, visit Vermont and create your own. ❖

<u>Above:</u> Pieces of Rocky Road Fudge.

ROCKY ROAD FUDGE

1   Cup miniature marshmallows
1   3.4 Ounce package JELL-O⁽ᴿ⁾ Brand chocolate cook and serve pudding mix
11/2 Cups granulated sugar
1   Tablespoon all natural butter-flavored sprinkles
1/2   Cup plus 2 Tablespoons evaporated skimmed milk
5   Cups miniature marshmallows
1   Tablespoon pecans, chopped

Except for the marshmallows and pecans, place ingredients in a 10" cast iron skillet. Place your stainless steel whisk next to the stove. Before we begin cooking the candy, let's prepare some other items.

Prepare a 7" by 10" by 2" (Approximately) pan or casserole dish by lining it with aluminum foil and spraying it with butter flavored vegetable spray. Measure out one cup of marshmallows and spread them evenly over the bottom of this pan or dish. Next, measure out 5 cups of marshmallows and set them in front of the hand mixer. You'll need several tablespoons so get them out and have them handy.

Ok, let's start cooking. Place skillet on a large electric burner which is set to the hottest temperature. If using a gas stove, turn it to full on. Mix and stir continously.

When mixture comes to a full rolling boil, set an accurate timer to 5 minutes and continue stirring.

After 5 minutes, remove the skillet from the hot burner and continue stirring until mixture no longer boils.

Add marshmallows and combine using a tablespoon to mix marshmallows and the hot mixture. You can't use the hand mixer at first because the melting marshmallows will climb up the beaters and refuse to come down. By using a tablespoon first the mixture is somewhat thinned and now you can use the hand mixer effectively. Mix until smooth and the marshmallows are melted. (About a minute or so)

Pour hot mixture on top of marshmallows in aluminum foil lined pan or dish. Sprinkle pecans on top and allow to firm up over night.

When set, use a thin bladed knife to score or cut the fudge. Cover with plastic wrap and store what's left after you have appropriately sampled your fudge. ❖

Everyone who likes bananas will love this fudge!

For the best flavor, be sure to use a ripe banana. A green banana will yield little flavor.

For a more subtle flavor you may omit the banana extract.

The wonderful cereal used here will add texture and tone down the sweetness.

This fudge is best eaten the first or second day. ❖

BANANAS, CREAM & CRUNCH FUDGE

1   3.0 Ounce package JELL-O⁽ᴿ⁾ Brand vanilla cook and serve pudding mix
11/2 Cups granulated sugar
1   Tablespoon all natural butter-flavored sprinkles
1/4   Cup plus 2 Tablespoons evaporated skimmed milk
1/2   Cup fresh, ripe bananas, finely mashed
1   Teaspoon banana extract
5   Cups miniature marshmallows
1   Cup Post⁽ᴿ⁾ Banana Nut Crunch⁽ᵀᴹ⁾ Cereal

Except for the marshmallows and cereal, place ingredients in a 10" cast iron skillet. Place your stainless steel whisk next to the stove. Before we begin cooking the candy, let's prepare some other items.

Prepare a plate or platter by spraying it with butter flavored vegetable spray and set it on a wire cooling rack. Next, measure the marshmallows and set them in front of the hand mixer. You'll need several tablespoons so get them out and have them handy.

Ok, let's start cooking. Place skillet on a large electric burner which is set to the hottest temperature. If using a gas stove, turn it to full on. Mix and stir continously.

When mixture comes to a full rolling boil, set an accurate timer to 5 minutes and continue stirring.

After 5 minutes, remove the skillet from the hot burner and continue stirring until mixture no longer boils.

Add marshmallows and combine using a tablespoon to mix marshmallows and the hot mixture. You can't use the hand mixer at first because the melting marshmallows will climb up the beaters and refuse to come down. By using a tablespoon first the mixture is somewhat thinned and now you can use the hand mixer effectively. Mix until smooth and the marshmallows are melted. (About a minute or so)

Add cereal, mix well with a tablespoon, and pour mixture out onto the veggie sprayed plate or platter and place it on a wire rack to cool.

Check your candy every few minutes by swirling the top. Shortly, (usually within 10 to 30 minutes) these swirls will begin to hold their shape. Apply your final pattern or design.

Use a butter knife to raise and shape the edges of your fudge. Remember, the outer edges will set up last.

When set, use a thin bladed knife to score or cut the fudge. Cover with plastic wrap and store what's left after you have appropriately sampled your fudge. ❖

On a warm summer day, prior to harvest, as you walk through a Missouri peach orchard, you can almost smell and taste the warm peach pies, the sweet jams and the cold home made peach ice cream.

To the list of peachy good things to eat you can now add this fudge. Just remember to eat it during the first couple of days and don't store it. ❖

Above: Peach Pecan Fudge

PEACH PECAN FUDGE

1   3.0 Ounce package JELL-O(R) Brand vanilla cook and serve pudding mix
11/2 Cups granulated sugar
1   Tablespoon all natural butter-flavored sprinkles
1/4   Cup plus 2 Tablespoons evaporated skimmed milk
1/4   Cup peach brandy
1   Teaspoon peach flavor
5   Cups miniature marshmallows
1   Cup Ralston(R) Brand Peach Muesli Cereal with Pecans

Except for the marshmallows and cereal, place ingredients in a 10" cast iron skillet. Place your stainless steel whisk next to the stove. Before we begin cooking the candy, let's prepare some other items.

Prepare a plate or platter by spraying it with butter flavored vegetable spray and set it on a wire cooling rack. Next, measure the marshmallows and set them in front of the hand mixer. You'll need several tablespoons so get them out and have them handy.

Ok, let's start cooking. Place skillet on a large electric burner which is set to the hottest temperature. If using a gas stove, turn it to full on. Mix and stir continously.

When mixture comes to a full rolling boil, set an accurate timer to 5 minutes and continue stirring.

After 5 minutes, remove the skillet from the hot burner and continue stirring until mixture no longer boils.

Add marshmallows and combine using a tablespoon to mix marshmallows and the hot mixture. You can't use the hand mixer at first because the melting marshmallows will climb up the beaters and refuse to come down. By using a tablespoon first the mixture is somewhat thinned and now you can use the hand mixer effectively. Mix until smooth and the marshmallows are melted. (About a minute or so)

Add cereal, mix well with a tablespoon, and pour mixture out onto the veggie sprayed plate or platter and place it on a wire rack to cool.

Check your candy every few minutes by swirling the top. Shortly, (usually within 10 to 30 minutes) these swirls will begin to hold their shape. Apply your final pattern or design.

Use a butter knife to raise and shape the edges of your fudge. Remember, the outer edges will set up last.

When set, use a thin bladed knife to score or cut the fudge. Cover with plastic wrap and store what's left after you have appropriately sampled your fudge. ❖

Originally, I was going to make this fudge a beginners fudge because it was so cooperative in setting-up properly and acting as a good fudge should. However, I looked a second time at the long list of ingredients and decided that perhaps it was a little bit too complex for a beginner.

Although the list of ingredients might look a little long you will be rewarded with the great flavors of maple, butter and vanilla coupled with the crunch of granola. Do these guys go together? Absolutely!

Best eaten the first day or two. ❖

MAPLE BUTTER NUT CRUNCH FUDGE

1	3 Ounce package JELL-O(R) Brand vanilla cook and serve pudding mix
1 1/2	Cups granulated sugar
2	Tablespoons all natural butter-flavored sprinkles
1/2	Cup plus 1 Tablespoon evaporated skimmed milk
1/4	Cup maple syrup
1	Teaspoon pecan flavor
1	Teaspoon maple flavor
5	Cups miniature marshmallows
2/3	Cup low-fat granola

Except for the marshmallows and the low-fat granola , place ingredients in a 10" cast iron skillet. Place your stainless steel whisk next to the stove. Before we begin cooking the candy, let's prepare some other items.

Prepare a plate or platter by spraying it with butter flavored vegetable spray and set it on a wire cooling rack. Next, measure the marshmallows and set them in front of the hand mixer. You'll need several tablespoons so get them out and have them handy.

Ok, let's start cooking. Place skillet on a large electric burner which is set to the hottest temperature. If using a gas stove, turn it to full on. Mix and stir continously.

When mixture comes to a full rolling boil, set an accurate timer to 5 minutes and continue stirring.

After 5 minutes, remove the skillet from the hot burner and continue stirring until mixture no longer boils.

Add marshmallows and combine using a tablespoon to mix marshmallows and the hot mixture. You can't use the hand mixer at first because the melting marshmallows will climb up the beaters and refuse to come down. By using a tablespoon first the mixture is somewhat thinned and now you can use the hand mixer effectively. Mix until smooth and the marshmallows are melted. (About a minute or so)

Add low-fat granola, mix well with a tablespoon, and pour mixture out onto the veggie sprayed plate or platter and place it on a wire rack to cool.

Check your candy every few minutes by swirling the top. Shortly, (usually within 10 to 30 minutes) these swirls will begin to hold their shape. Apply your final pattern or design. Use a butter knife to raise and shape the edges. Remember, the outer edges will set up last.

When set, use a thin bladed knife to score or cut the fudge. Cover with plastic wrap and store what's left after you have appropriately sampled your fudge. ❖

Mother said,"Crack them black walnuts and we'll make some fudge".

All of us children were eager to smack them walnuts with a hammer, even though the likelihood of a mashed finger was probable. You see:

> Black walnuts are onery critters,
> That are hard to crack.
> The nut meats are difficult to glean,
> And so for this reason I have chosen to use,
> An extract instead of the real thing.

Another reason for using an extract is the fact that real black walnuts are loaded with fat. ❖

BUTTERED BLACK WALNUT FUDGE

1	3.0 Ounce package JELL-O(R) Brand vanilla cook and serve pudding mix
13/4	Cups granulated sugar
1	Tablespoon all natural butter-flavored sprinkles
1	Teaspoon black walnut extract
1/2	Cup plus 2 Tablespoons evaporated skimmed milk
2/3	Cup "Nut Meats", chopped, from page 25
5	Cups miniature marshmallows

Except for the marshmallows, place ingredients in a 10" cast iron skillet. Place your stainless steel whisk next to the stove. Before we begin cooking the candy, let's prepare some other items.

Prepare a plate or platter by spraying it with butter flavored vegetable spray and set it on a wire cooling rack. Next, measure the marshmallows and set them in front of the hand mixer. You'll need several tablespoons so get them out and have them handy.

Ok, let's start cooking. Place skillet on a large electric burner which is set to the hottest temperature. If using a gas stove, turn it to full on. Mix and stir continously.

When mixture comes to a full rolling boil, set an accurate timer to 5 minutes and continue stirring.

After 5 minutes, remove the skillet from the hot burner and continue stirring until mixture no longer boils.

Add marshmallows and combine using a tablespoon to mix marshmallows and the hot mixture. You can't use the hand mixer at first because the melting marshmallows will climb up the beaters and refuse to come down. By using a tablespoon first the mixture is somewhat thinned and now you can use the hand mixer effectively. Mix until smooth and the marshmallows are melted. (About a minute or so)

Pour mixture out onto the veggie sprayed plate or platter and place it on a wire rack to cool.

Check your candy every few minutes by swirling the top. Shortly, (usually within 10 to 30 minutes) these swirls will begin to hold their shape. Apply your final pattern or design.

Use a butter knife to raise and shape the edges of your fudge. Remember, the outer edges will set up last.

When set, use a thin bladed knife to score or cut the fudge. Cover with plastic wrap and store what's left after you have appropriately sampled your fudge. ❖

Years ago, I used to wander the back acres of our Missouri farm, closely monitoring the hazelnut bushes. These nuts were my favorites because of the ease in cracking and removing that lucious kernel of goodness. They were much easier to eat than the black walnuts or hickory nuts that were in abundance. I quickly discovered that there were other eyes watching those nuts much more carefully than mine. I learned that, as the hazelnuts ripened, they were quickly harvested --- by the squirrels!

Rarely did they leave me any nuts.

Much to my surprise I discovered the same wonderful flavor of those hazelnuts bottled up in a lively liqueur named Frangelico. I hope you enjoy the pristine flavors in this fudge. ❖

HAZELNUT FUDGE

1   3.0 Ounce package JELL-O(R) Brand vanilla cook and serve pudding mix
11/2 Cups granulated sugar
2   Tablespoons instant non fat dry milk powder
1   Tablespoon all natural butter-flavored sprinkles
1/4   Cup evaporated skimmed milk
1/3   Cup Frangelico liqueur
2/3   Cup "Nut Meats", chopped, from page 25
5   Cups miniature marshmallows

<u>Except for the marshmallows</u>, place ingredients in a 10" cast iron skillet. Place your stainless steel whisk next to the stove. Before we begin cooking the candy, let's prepare some other items.

Prepare a plate or platter by spraying it with butter flavored vegetable spray and set it on a wire cooling rack. Next, measure the marshmallows and set them in front of the hand mixer. You'll need several tablespoons so get them out and have them handy.

Ok, let's start cooking. Place skillet on a large electric burner which is set to the hottest temperature. If using a gas stove, turn it to full on. Mix and stir continously.

When mixture comes to a full rolling boil, set an accurate timer to 5 minutes and continue stirring.

After 5 minutes, remove the skillet from the hot burner and continue stirring until mixture no longer boils.

Add marshmallows and combine using a tablespoon to mix marshmallows and the hot mixture. You can't use the hand mixer at first because the melting marshmallows will climb up the beaters and refuse to come down. By using a tablespoon first the mixture is somewhat thinned and now you can use the hand mixer effectively. Mix until smooth and the marshmallows are melted. (About a minute or so)

Pour mixture out onto the veggie sprayed plate or platter and place it on a wire rack to cool.

Check your candy every few minutes by swirling the top. Shortly, (usually within 10 to 30 minutes) these swirls will begin to hold their shape. Apply your final pattern or design.

Use a butter knife to raise and shape the edges of your fudge. Remember, the outer edges will set up last.

When set, use a thin bladed knife to score or cut the fudge. Cover with plastic wrap and store what's left after you have appropriately sampled your fudge. ❖

It probably first happened on one of Captain Cook's early visits to the Pacific Islands. A native Islander likely demonstrated the technique involved in harvesting the tasty milk from a coconut. An Able-Seaman conceivably decided that the coconut milk was a little too bland for his taste buds and so he added his daily ration of Kill Devil Rum to the milky liquid.

Ever since that long ago time, whenever a sailor has coconut milk and rum, he mixes them together, sits back in the shade and partakes of this flavorful blend.

Raisin Note:

For Coconut Rum Raisin Fudge replace the shredded coconut with 1/2 cup of raisins. This will lower the fat content and give you a new flavor.

Above: Coconut Rum Fudge with 1 tablespoon of the coconut called for in the recipe, reserved, toasted and used as a top dressing.

COCONUT RUM FUDGE

1   3 Ounce package JELL-O⁽ᴿ⁾ Brand vanilla cook and serve pudding mix
11/2 Cups granulated sugar
1   Tablespoon all natural butter-flavored sprinkles
6   Tablespoons flake coconut
1/4 Cup plus 1 Tablespoon evaporated skimmed milk
1/4 Cup dark rum
1   Teaspoon rum flavor
1   Teaspoon coconut extract
5   Cups miniature marshmallows

Except for the marshmallows, place ingredients in a 10" cast iron skillet. Place your stainless steel whisk next to the stove. Before we begin cooking the candy, let's prepare some other items.

Prepare a plate or platter by spraying it with butter flavored vegetable spray and set it on a wire cooling rack. Next, measure the marshmallows and set them in front of the hand mixer. You'll need several tablespoons so get them out and have them handy.

Ok, let's start cooking. Place skillet on a large electric burner which is set to the hottest temperature. If using a gas stove, turn it to full on. Mix and stir continously.

When mixture comes to a full rolling boil, set an accurate timer to 5 minutes and continue stirring. ❀ After 5 minutes, remove from the hot burner and continue stirring until mixture no longer boils.

Add marshmallows and combine using a tablespoon to mix marshmallows and the hot mixture. You can't use the hand mixer at first because the melting marshmallows will climb up the beaters and refuse to come down. By using a tablespoon first the mixture is somewhat thinned and now you can use the hand mixer effectively. Mix until smooth and the marshmallows are melted. (About a minute or so)

Pour mixture out onto the veggie sprayed plate or platter and place it on a wire rack to cool.

Check your candy every few minutes by swirling the top. Shortly, (usually within 10 to 30 minutes) these swirls will begin to hold their shape. Apply your final pattern or design.

Use a butter knife to raise and shape the edges of your fudge. Remember, the outer edges will set up last.

When set, use a thin bladed knife to score or cut the fudge. Cover with plastic wrap and store what's left after you have appropriately sampled your fudge. ❖

When I first made this fudge I was merely investigating potential textures and flavors. What I discovered was a coconut macaroon fudge!

You have to put such a discovery in the proper perspective. Understand that I had not eaten a fat-filled macaroon in years. Further understand that I loved the taste and texture of a fancy coconut macaroon. Now can you imagine the grin on my face as I bit into this fudge for the **second** time?

The first bite brought disbelief and a blank stare.

This fudge should be eaten and not stored as the bran flakes will become chewy after a few days, however chewy is still good. ❖

COCONUT MACAROON FUDGE

1   3 Ounce package JELL-O⁽ᴿ⁾ Brand vanilla cook and serve pudding mix
11/2 Cups granulated sugar
1   Tablespoon all natural butter-flavored sprinkles
6   Tablespoons shredded coconut
1/2   Cup plus 1 Tablespoons evaporated skimmed milk
1   Teaspoon coconut extract
1   Teaspoon rum flavor
5   Cups miniature marshmallows
1   Cup oat bran flakes

Except for the marshmallows and the oat bran flakes, place ingredients in a 10" cast iron skillet. Place your stainless steel whisk next to the stove. Before we begin cooking the candy, let's prepare some other items.

Prepare a plate or platter by spraying it with butter flavored vegetable spray and set it on a wire cooling rack. Next, measure the marshmallows and set them in front of the hand mixer. You'll need several tablespoons so get them out and have them handy.

Ok, let's start cooking. Place skillet on a large electric burner which is set to the hottest temperature. If using a gas stove, turn it to full on. Mix and stir continously.

When mixture comes to a full rolling boil, set an accurate timer to 5 minutes and continue stirring. ❀ After 5 minutes, remove the skillet from the hot burner and continue stirring until the mixture no longer boils.

Add marshmallows and combine using a tablespoon to mix marshmallows and the hot mixture. You can't use the hand mixer at first because the melting marshmallows will climb up the beaters and refuse to come down. By using a tablespoon first the mixture is somewhat thinned and now you can use the hand mixer effectively. Mix until smooth and the marshmallows are melted. (About a minute or so)

Add oat bran flakes, mix well with a tablespoon, and pour mixture out onto the veggie sprayed plate or platter and place it on a wire rack to cool.

Check your candy every few minutes by swirling the top. Shortly, (usually within 10 to 30 minutes) these swirls will begin to hold their shape. Apply your final pattern or design.

Use a butter knife to raise and shape the edges of your fudge. Remember, the outer edges will set up last.

When set, use a thin bladed knife to score or cut the fudge. Cover with plastic wrap and store what's left after you have appropriately sampled your fudge.❖

Good fudge never spoils when properly eaten.

EPILOGUE

The mental processes involved in eating this no-fat fudge closely approximates the following communication:

Brain to Eye
>Is that fudge?

Eye to Brain
>It appears so.

Brain to Hand
>Pick a piece up.

Hand to Brain
>OK, I have; What now?

Brain to Mouth
>Let's bite it.

Mouth to Brain
>I have and it feels like fudge.

Brain to tongue
>Let's taste it.

Tongue to Brain
>It's sweet and flavorful, like fudge.

Brain to all systems
>Let's consume the fudge.

Brain to all systems
>The fudge was good so let's eat some more.

Brain to all systems
>Second piece was good. Since sugar is the
>only fuel I burn, let's have another piece.

Stomach to Brain
>I'm getting sick!

Brain to Stomach
>Just one more piece.

Stomach to Brain
>I'm really going to be sick!

The moral of this story is this: No-fat fudge is thousands of times better for you than regular fat fudge but you still shouldn't overdose on it. ❖

COPYRIGHT & TRADEMARK
ACKNOWLEDGMENT

INDEX

My Favorite Recipes

Notes

Norman Rose

has been writing about and teaching no fat cooking for years. At colleges, hospitals, senior centers, churches, schools, and corporations, Mr. Rose has been actively and eagerly showing folks how to take the guilt out of a fun thing------EATING!

As an engineer, research and development specialist, teacher, restaurateur, lecturer, and documentary producer, Mr. Rose has now taken on the task of promoting the necessity of fat free cooking, eating and -----------------------ENJOYING!

His first book, <u>NO FAT PLEASE</u>, has been labeled as one of America's best selling underground books, because of word-of-mouth sales from across the country.

His second book, <u>JUST NO FAT</u>, was considered THE standard within the industry for no fat cooking of regular food for regular people until his third book, <u>FAVORITE FOODS:NO FAT COOKING</u>, hit the national scene in May, 1994 (Published by WRS Publishing, Waco Texas). It is this latter book containing the 10 master tips to no fat cooking that will be used as a high school text book in 1995.

This his fourth book, <u>NO FAT FUDGE</u>, published October 1, 1994 has been called an unbelievable work in which Mr. Rose shows the reader how to celebrate America's favorite candy without the fat! In words and pictures folks learn a much simpler, quicker method to prepare great fudge. Recipes vary from straight forward fudges such as Chocolate, "Peanut Butter", Vanilla, German Chocolate, Coconut Rum and Coconut Macaroon to the delightful chapter on Holiday Fudge, Bon Bons & Truffles, all without the fat. The chapter, "For Little Hands", with its attendant "Fudgkins", becomes a tradition in the making.

For more information telephone 1-913 384 9246 or write to:

Norman Rose
P. O. Box 8009
Shawnee Mission, Kansas
66208
⌘

Chapter on Desserts Seems Like Getting Away With Murder

Favorite Foods: No Fat Cooking

By: Norman Rose
Foreword by Wayman Spence, M.D.

* Over 400 low-fat recipes of regular foods for regular people.

* Less filling, tastes great

About the book:
Readers already know that fat is bad, and why. This cookbook gets right to the point and tells them how to get around it-to have their cake and eat it too. These recipes include all the kinds of foods people are used to eating, from cheeseburgers to cherry pies-they just use different ingredients. These recipes give very tasty results and they're so "cooker-friendly" they're easy to stick to.

Norman Rose's first book, **No Fat Please**, has been labeled as one of America's best-selling underground books, primarily because of word-of-mouth sales across the country. Rose, a sought-after speaker on the subject, himself has been a patient in the Kansas City Lipid and Atherosclerosis Prevention Clinic for some time. His father had his first heart attack at age 35, and Norman was smart enough to realize that, with his family history, he'd better learn a new way of cooking and eating. The book covers every type of recipe from appetizers, to soups, to ethnic foods, to breads, to desserts - plus much, much more.

About the author:
Norman Rose, a former rocket scientist for the Navy and currently an engineer, teacher, producer, author and restaurateur, has taken on the task of promoting fat-free cooking. Norman lives and cooks with his wife, Brenda, in Prairie Village, Kansas, a suburb of Kansas City.

May-94   6 1/8 X 9 1/8
360 pages   Illustrated
Cloth   1-56796-039-1
Cookbook/Nutrition/Health